Macmillan
Work Out
Series

Work Out

Geography

GCSE

# The titles in this series

**For examinations at 16+**

Accounting
Biology
Business Studies
Chemistry
Computer Studies
Economics
English
French
Geography
German

Graphic Communication
Human Biology
Mathematics
Numeracy
Physics
Social and Economic History
Sociology
Spanish
Statistics

**For examinations at 'A' Level**

Accounting
Applied Mathematics
Biology
Chemistry
Economics

English Literature
French
Physics
Pure Mathematics
Statistics

**For examinations at college level**

Dynamics
Electromagnetic Fields
Electronics
Elements of Banking
Engineering Thermodynamics

Fluid Mechanics
Mathematics for Economists
Operational Research
Organic Chemistry
Waves and Optics

MACMILLAN
WORK OUT
SERIES

# Work Out

# Geography

# GCSE

## P. N. Harper

MACMILLAN

First published 1989

Published by
MACMILLAN EDUCATION LTD
Houndmills, Basingstoke, Hampshire RG21 2XS
and London
Companies and representatives
throughout the world

Editorial and production by Hart McLeod, Cambridge

Printed in Hong Kong

British Library Cataloguing in Publication Data
Harper, P.
Work out geography GCSE (Macmillan work out series)
1. England. Secondary schools. Curriculum subjects: Geography.
GCSE examinations. Techniques
I. Title
910′.76
ISBN 0–333–46531–8

For Roz, Katie and Thomas

# Contents

# Acknowledgements

There are four examining groups in England, each with several constituent examining boards. Separate examining boards exist for Wales and Northern Ireland. The addresses of the boards responsible for GCSE Geography syllabuses are as follows:

*London and East Anglian Group*, The Lindens, Lexden Road, Colchester, Essex CO3 3RL

*Midland Examining Group*, Robins Wood House, Robins Wood Road, Aspley, Nottingham NG8 3NR

*Northern Examining Association* (NEA, A and B), 12 Harter Street, Manchester M1 6HL

*Northern Examining Association* (NEA, C and D), 31–33 Springfield Avenue, Harrogate HG1 2HW

*Southern Examining Group* (SEG A), 23–29 Marsh Street, Bristol BS1 4BP

*Southern Examining Group* (SEG B), Beloe House, 2–4 Mount Ephraim Road, Royal Tunbridge Wells, Kent TN1 1EU

*Welsh Joint Education Committee*, 245 Western Avenue, Cardiff CF5 2YX

*Northern Ireland Schools Examinations Council*, Beechill House, 42 Beechill Road, Belfast BT8 4RS

The author and publishers wish to thank the following who have kindly given permission for the use of copyright material:

East Anglian Examinations Board, Northern Ireland Schools Examinations Council and Southern Examining Group for questions from previously published examination papers; the *Oxford Times* for extracts from 'M-way property boom predicted' by Phil Taylor, 20.3.87; Oxford University Press for an illustration from *Development in the Third World* by Michael Morrish; Aerofilms (pages 81, 84, 85); British Rail (page 154); Cambridge University Collection (page 64); J. Allan Cash (page 113, cover: sand dunes in Death Valley, California); M. M. Kaunda (page 184, middle right); Macmillan Photo Records/Eastern Nigeria Information Service (page 184); Macmillan Photo Research/Northern Nigeria Information Service (page 184); Ministry of Local Government and Information, Nigeria (page 184); Ordnance Survey (final page).

Every effort has been made to trace all the copyright holders, but if any have been inadvertently overlooked the publishers will be pleased to make the necessary arrangements at the first opportunity.

# 1 Introduction

## 1.1 The structure of this book

This book is divided into 13 chapters. Chapter 1 explains how to use this book. Chapter 2 gives advice on how to approach the coursework section of GCSE. Chapters 3 to 13 begin with course notes which cover the main topics of the GCSE examination. In most chapters the notes are followed firstly by multiple choice and completion questions, and secondly by structured questions and solutions; the answers to the multiple-choice and completion questions make up the final section of each chapter.

## 1.2 How to use the course notes

1. The course notes include definitions of key terms, text, diagrams and tables that summarise the geography of a particular topic.
2. These notes are designed to be used during your two-year course to help you summarise the main ideas and to help you revise at the end of the course prior to the examination.
3. Some questions in the examination will ask you to give examples. The last section of the notes is a table of examples that you should complete after you have studied a particular topic with your teacher.

## 1.3 How to use the multiple-choice and completion questions

Although only two syllabuses (LEAG syllabus A and NEA syllabus A) use this type of question it is important that you complete the questions as they provide a quick way of testing yourself both during the course and while you are revising.

## 1.4 How to use the structured questions

1. Most of the chapters have two or three structured questions. You should complete some of the questions during your two-year course and save some until you begin to revise.
2. When you have completed a question you should compare your answer with the suggested solution.

## 1.5 The content of the book and your syllabus

1. It is important that you find out which GCSE syllabus you are following, as the content varies from one syllabus to another.

2. Table 1.1 sets out the content of the book and suggests which sections need to be studied by students who are following a particular syllabus. Take a careful note of the sections that you need to study.

**Table 1.1**  Suggestions on how the content of the book relates to the content of the different syllabuses

| Summary of chapter content | NEA A | NEA B | NEA C | NEA D | MEG A | MEG B | MEG C | MEG D* | MEG/WJEC E | LEAG A | LEAG B | LEAG D | WJEC | NISEC | SEG A1 and A2 | SEG B |
|---|---|---|---|---|---|---|---|---|---|---|---|---|---|---|---|---|
| **2 Coursework** | • | • | • | • | • | • | • | • | • | • | • | • | • | • | • | • |
| **3 The Structure of the Earth** | | | | | | | | | | | | | | | | |
| The earth's structure | | | | • | | • | | | | | | | | • | • | |
| Earth movements | | | • | • | • | • | | • | | | | | | • | • | |
| The effect on people of earthquakes and volcanoes | • | | • | | | • | • | • | | | | | | | • | • |
| **4 Weather, Climate and Ecosystems** | | | | | | | | | | | | | | | | |
| Weather and climate | | | | • | | | | • | | • | | • | • | • | • | |
| Weather as a hazard | • | | • | | • | • | | • | | • | | | • | | | • |
| Ecosystems | | | • | | | • | • | | | • | • | • | • | • | | |
| **5 Shaping the Landscape** | | | | | | | | | | | | | | | | |
| Earth shaping processes | • | | | • | • | • | | | • | | | • | • | | • | • |
| The drainage system | • | • | • | • | • | • | • | • | • | • | • | • | • | • | • | • |
| **6 Natural Resources** | • | • | • | • | | | • | • | | • | • | • | | • | | |
| **7 Population** | | | | | | | | | | | | | | | | |
| Distribution and density | • | • | • | • | • | • | | • | | • | | • | • | • | • | |
| Population growth | • | • | • | • | • | • | | | | • | | • | • | • | • | |
| Migration | • | • | • | • | • | • | | • | | • | | • | • | • | | • |
| **8 Settlement** | | | | | | | | | | | | | | | | |
| Growth and decline of settlements | • | • | • | • | • | • | • | • | • | • | • | • | • | • | • | • |
| Urban structure | • | • | • | • | • | • | • | • | • | • | • | • | • | • | • | • |
| Settlement problems | • | • | | | | | • | • | • | • | • | • | • | • | • | • |
| **9 Development** | | | | | | | | | | | | | | | | |
| Measuring development | | | • | • | • | | • | | | | | | • | • | • | • |
| Barriers to development | | • | • | • | • | | • | • | | • | • | | • | • | • | • |
| Regional development | • | • | • | • | • | | • | • | | • | • | • | | • | • | • |

| Topic | 1 | 2 | 3 | 4 | 5 | 6 | 7 | 8 | 9 | 10 | 11 | 12 | 13 | 14 | 15 | 16 |
|---|---|---|---|---|---|---|---|---|---|---|---|---|---|---|---|---|
| **10 Transport** | | | | | | | | | | | | | | | | |
| Transport networks | | • | | | | | • | • | • | | • | | • | | | |
| Modes of transport | | • | | | | | • | • | • | | • | | • | | | |
| Transport problems | | • | • | | | | • | • | • | | • | | • | | | |
| **11 Agriculture** | | | | | | | | | | | | | | | | |
| Agriculture as a system | • | • | • | • | • | • | | • | | • | • | • | • | • | • | • |
| The decision-making process | • | • | • | • | • | • | | • | | • | • | • | • | • | • | • |
| Contrasts in agriculture | • | • | | • | • | • | | • | | • | • | • | • | • | • | • |
| Agriculture and the environment | • | • | • | • | • | • | | • | | • | • | • | • | • | • | • |
| **12 Secondary Industry** | | | | | | | | | | | | | | | | |
| The characteristics of secondary industry | • | • | • | • | • | • | | • | • | • | • | • | • | • | • | • |
| Industrial change, industrial location | • | • | • | • | • | • | • | • | • | • | • | • | • | • | • | • |
| Industrial pollution | • | • | • | • | • | • | | • | • | • | • | • | • | • | • | • |
| **13 Tertiary Industry** | | | | | | | | | | | | | | | | |
| The growth of tertiary industry | • | • | • | • | • | • | | • | • | • | • | • | • | • | | • |
| Industrial location | • | • | • | • | • | • | • | • | • | • | • | • | • | • | | • |
| The tourist industry | • | • | • | • | | | | • | | • | | | | | | • |

*This syllabus allows a school to choose the content. Get a copy of the school syllabus from your teacher.

# 2 Coursework

## 2.1 Types of coursework

### (a) Coursework

1. During your two-year course you will do some pieces of work which are marked by your teacher and which count towards your final GCSE grade; this work is called coursework.
2. The grade that you get for your GCSE will depend on how well you do in the coursework as well as the examination at the end of your course.

### (b) The Importance of Coursework

1. The percentage of marks given to coursework varies from syllabus to syllabus.

**Table 2.1** Percentage of the total GCSE marks given for coursework

| Examination group | Syllabus | Percentage of total GCSE for coursework |
|---|---|---|
| NEA | A | 25 |
| | B | 25 or 60* |
| | C | 30 |
| | D | 50 |
| SEG | A | 25 |
| | B | 40 |
| NISEC | | 20 |
| LEAG | A | 30 |
| | B | 40 |
| | D | 25 |
| MEG | A | 25 |
| | B | 28 |
| | C | 50 |
| | D | 50 |
| MEG/WJEC joint | E | 40 |
| WJEC | | 20 |

*60% if optional course tests are used

2. Even the lowest figure of 20% is still a large proportion of the final mark, so it is important to do as well as you can in the coursework as it will influence your final grade.
3. Coursework is also important because it tests various abilities in a different way to the final examination. You may be better at coursework than at the examination where you are tested in a strict and short time limit.

### (c) Differences between Syllabuses

1. The type of coursework that you will be asked to do varies from syllabus to syllabus.

**Table 2.2** Types of coursework

| Examination Group | Syllabus | Enquiry | Exercises | Tests |
|---|---|---|---|---|
| NEA | A | 1 or more | | |
| | B | 1 or more | | 4 (optional) |
| | C | 2 | | |
| | D | 1 or 2 | 3 | |
| SEG | A | 1 | | |
| | B | 1 | 2 | |
| NISEC | | 1 | | |
| LEAG | A | 2 | | |
| | B | 3 | | |
| | D | 1 | | |
| MEG | A | 1 or 2 or 3 | | |
| | B | 1 or 2 or 3 | | |
| | C | 2 | 2 | |
| | D | 1 or 2 | 3 | |
| MEG/WJEC joint | E | 1 | 2 | |
| WJEC | | 1 | | |

2. As you can see from Table 2.2 the main type of coursework is some form of geographical enquiry. The rest of this chapter concentrates on how you should approach an enquiry.
3. An individual study, a geographical investigation and a course study are three other names given to a geographical enquiry.

## 2.2 Choosing a topic for geographical enquiry

### (a) Topic Choice

1. Choosing a suitable topic for enquiry is possibly the most important part of your coursework, as it will be very difficult to show how good you are at geography if you choose an unsuitable topic.
2. Fig. 2.1 sets out the questions that you should ask yourself about your possible choice of topic, and the rest of this section develops the questions.

**Figure 2.1**   Some questions to ask when thinking about topic choice

3. The answer to some of these questions will vary depending on the syllabus that you are doing. Listen very carefully when your teacher introduces the enquiry to you.
4. By answering the questions you will become familiar with what your syllabus requires, and you will have planned your enquiry thoroughly. This will make the enquiry easier to write.

### (b) Free Choice

1. Some syllabuses allow you to choose any geographical topic.
2. Usually you will have to choose a topic which is related to one or more of the key ideas listed in your syllabus.

### (c) Topic Interest

As you will be spending a number of weeks on your enquiry, try to choose a topic that interests you.

6

## (d) Marking Scheme

1. Each syllabus sets out a marking scheme that will be used by your teacher to award you a mark.
2. They are often complicated but you should try to identify and understand the key words in the scheme. If you are unsure how your enquiry will be marked, then ask your teacher. When the enquiry is complete it is too late to realise that you have ignored some of the key words in the marking scheme.
3. Keep the key words of the marking scheme in your mind while you are planning your enquiry. When you have finished your plan, check that you will have covered all the key words when your enquiry is complete. If you haven't, go back and adapt your plan.

**Table 2.3**  An example of an enquiry marking scheme

| *Criteria for assessment of geographical enquiries* | *Marks* |
| --- | --- |
| 1. **Collection** of **primary data** and, where appropriate, supporting **secondary data relevant** to a topic. | 12 |
| 2. **Presentation** of data using a **variety** of **geographically appropriate** forms. | 12 |
| 3. **Analysis** and **interpretation** of **data** by application of geographical **concepts** and **principles**, including identification of **values** and their role in decision-making. | 14 |
| 4. **Conclusions** drawn from the **findings** of the enquiries, including, where appropriate, **proposals**, **justifications** and **evaluations for solutions** to geographical problems. | 12 |
| | 50 |

MEG syllabus A

## (e) Enquiry Route

1. An enquiry route simply divides the whole enquiry into different stages and tells you which stage to do first, second etc.
2. Most syllabuses suggest and some insist that your enquiry title should be either a question, a hypothesis or a problem to investigate. Many syllabuses then set out an enquiry route, similar to the example in Fig. 2.2.
3. Following an enquiry route will help you organise your enquiry and ensure that you don't miss out any important stages.
4. Before you decide finally on your topic you should go through the first few stages of the enquiry route to see if your topic allows you to follow it (see Table 2.4).
5. If you find that your topic doesn't fit any of these stages, choose a new topic and try again.

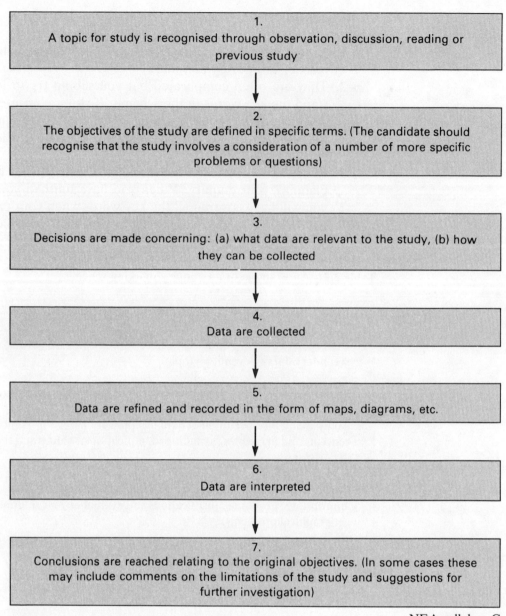

| 1. |
|---|
| A topic for study is recognised through observation, discussion, reading or previous study |

| 2. |
|---|
| The objectives of the study are defined in specific terms. (The candidate should recognise that the study involves a consideration of a number of more specific problems or questions) |

| 3. |
|---|
| Decisions are made concerning: (a) what data are relevant to the study, (b) how they can be collected |

| 4. |
|---|
| Data are collected |

| 5. |
|---|
| Data are refined and recorded in the form of maps, diagrams, etc. |

| 6. |
|---|
| Data are interpreted |

| 7. |
|---|
| Conclusions are reached relating to the original objectives. (In some cases these may include comments on the limitations of the study and suggestions for further investigation) |

NEA syllabus C

**Figure 2.2**  An example of an enquiry route

**Table 2.4**  Deciding if a topic fits the enquiry route

| Stage of enquiry in Fig 2.2 | Questions to ask |
|---|---|
| Stage 1 | Can I make a question or hypothesis based on this topic? Can I identify a problem connected to the topic? If I can do all three, which one should I choose? |
| Stage 2 | Can I say clearly why I am answering this question, proving or disproving this hypothesis or investigating this problem? |
| Stage 3 | What data do I need to collect to answer this question, prove or disprove this hypothesis or investigate this problem? Will some of this data mean that I have to do some fieldwork? (All syllabuses say that some part of the coursework must involve collecting data in the field.) Is the data that I need available? Can I collect it? |

## (f) Time Available

1. It is important that the question, hypothesis or problem that you have chosen can be completed in the time available.
2. The quality of the coursework that you have to do for other subjects may go down and your relaxation time may disappear if you attempt coursework that is too long.
3. Some syllabuses give guidance on the amount of time to be spent on an enquiry while others give the approximate number of words that you need to write. Your teacher will also give you guidance and may set a deadline for your enquiry to be handed in. Follow this guidance as it is designed to help you.
4. Once you have planned your enquiry you should be able to estimate how much time you will take. Try filling in Table 2.5.

**Table 2.5** Estimating the time that the enquiry will take

| Stage | Activity | Time estimate |
|---|---|---|
| Initial planning | One or two hours should be long enough, but don't rush this stage as a well planned enquiry will save time later on. | |
| Collecting the data | Work out how many visits you will need to make. How long will each one take? How much research will you need to do? | |
| Presenting the data | How many graphs, maps etc. will be needed? How long will each of them take to draw? | |
| Interpretation, evaluation and conclusions | Difficult to estimate but remember that a large percentage of the marks will be available for these sections. How much time have you got left after you have collected and presented the data? As a rough guide it should be at least 25% of the total time available. | |

5. If, after you have looked at the time that your enquiry will take, you find that either you have not enough time to interpret, evaluate and conclude or the whole enquiry is going to take too long, then you can try three remedies:

   (a) Look carefully at your question, hypothesis or problem to see if it can be narrowed down. For instance, the question 'How and why does traffic congestion vary from time to time and place to place in town X?' could be altered to 'How and why does traffic congestion vary from time to time at point Y in town X?'
   (b) Look carefully at the data that you are going to collect and present. Do you need it all or will your enquiry be as good if you leave some out?

(c) Sample the topic by an appropriate sampling technique. The question 'How and why does the sphere of influence of shops in the centre of city X vary?' could involve a large amount of time-consuming data collection unless the shops are sampled (e.g. collect data from one shop in ten).

## 2.3 Collecting the data

### (a) In the Classroom

1. If you have planned your enquiry well you should have decided how you are going to collect the data that you need.
2. Before you carry out any fieldwork, prepare a recording sheet for each set of data that you are going to collect. The record sheet should have clear spaces for you to record the data neatly so that when you come to process it, at a later date, it is easily understood.
3. Check any recording instruments that you are going to use, to make sure they work.

### (b) In the Field

1. Observe and record carefully to reduce the chance of errors.
2. Make detailed notes of any problems that you find, as these need to be written about later.

## 2.4 Writing up the coursework

### (a) The Layout

1. Your enquiry should begin with a table of contents which includes the headings of the different sections with their page numbers.
2. If you are following an enquiry route, then it is wise to use the different stages of the route as your main headings. These main headings can then be further divided into subheadings.

### (b) The Introduction

1. The introduction should set out clearly the title of the enquiry and say why you are going to study it. (Usually you will be studying the topic because you don't yet know the answer to a question, whether a hypothesis is true or false or the nature, extent and solution of a particular problem.)
2. Sometimes you may have some knowledge about the topic from what other people have written. The introduction could be used to summarise what you have read and the enquiry could then compare what you find with this summary, as your main aim or one of your aims.
3. The introduction should also set out briefly how you are going to proceed in the rest of the enquiry.
4. The title and purpose of the enquiry should be in your mind while you are doing the rest of the enquiry. Keep asking yourself if what you are drawing or writing is helping you to answer the question, prove or disprove the hypothesis or investigate the problem.

### (c) Methods of Data Collection

1. Briefly outline the data that you collected and describe the methods that you used.
2. Explain how you hoped that each set of data would help you and why you chose one method of collection rather than another.

### (d) Presentation of the Data

1. Each piece of relevant data that you have collected should be transcribed so that it is more easily understood.

**Table 2.6** Presentation techniques

| Maps | Graphs | Others |
|---|---|---|
| Choropleth | Line | Photographs |
| Isopleth | Bar | Plans |
| Topological | Radial | Diagrams |
| Sketch | Pie | Tables |
| | Triangular | |
| | Scatter | |

2. Often a set of data can be presented in a variety of ways. Think carefully about the alternatives and choose the method which shows a set of data to the best effect.
3. Each graph, map etc. should have a title, be neatly drawn and be given a number (e.g. Map 1) so that you can refer to it easily when you are writing.
4. If you have copied a map, graph, diagram etc. you should say clearly where it came from.
5. Most mark schemes require a variety of techniques of presentation to be used, but remember that if you want to compare two sets of data directly it is better to use the same presentation technique.

### (e) Interpretation and Explanation

1. For each graph, map etc. you need to:

   (a) describe the trends, patterns and relationships that it shows;
   (b) explain why it shows these trends, patterns and relationships;
   (c) explain how it relates to the title of your enquiry (how does it help you to answer the question, prove or disprove the hypothesis, investigate the problem?).

2. Often a piece of data that you present is related to other pieces of data. Write about the relationships and don't be afraid to write about contradictions (e.g. one piece of data may help you prove a hypothesis while another tends to disprove it).
3. If you feel that a set of data may be biased, then explain your reasons. The problems that you noted while doing your fieldwork may be useful here.

## (f) Conclusions

1. The conclusion should give your final view on the question, hypothesis or problem contained in the title (e.g. the hypothesis is true/partly true/ untrue).
2. Your final view should be supported by a summary of what you have already written and should not be based on new data or points of view that you have not discussed earlier (e.g. the hypothesis is true because of the information gained from the following sets of data . . .).
3. If you have observed any bias in your data you should state how this has influenced your final view.
4. You can also explain how you would like to remove any bias and how you would apply your results and develop the enquiry further.

# 3 The Structure of the Earth

## 3.1 The earth's structure

### (a) Inside the Earth

Four layers can be recognised:

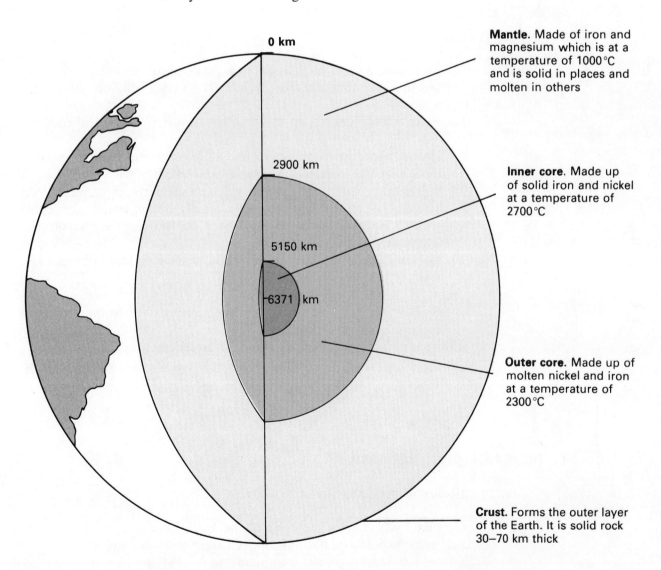

**Mantle.** Made of iron and magnesium which is at a temperature of 1000°C and is solid in places and molten in others

**Inner core.** Made up of solid iron and nickel at a temperature of 2700°C

**Outer core.** Made up of molten nickel and iron at a temperature of 2300°C

**Crust.** Forms the outer layer of the Earth. It is solid rock 30–70 km thick

0 km
2900 km
5150 km
6371 km

**Figure 3.1** Inside the earth

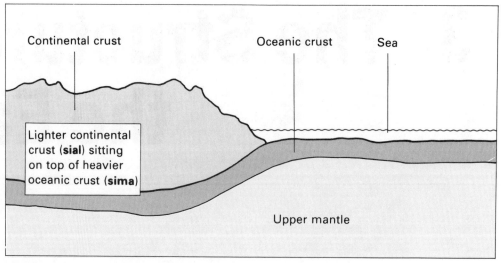

**Figure 3.2** The earth's crust

**(b) The Earth's Crust**

1. The crust of the earth or *lithosphere* is made up of dense oceanic crust and less dense continental crust which sits on top of the oceanic crust.

2. The earth's crust is made up of a number of different types of rock:

   (a) **Igneous rocks** are formed when the molten material from the mantle cools near the surface (e.g. granite and basalt).
   (b) **Sedimentary rocks** are formed when small particles of weathered material or shells are deposited, usually under water, and compressed as more layers are deposited on top (e.g. sandstone and limestone).
   (c) **Metamorphic rocks** are formed when heat or pressure changes the rocks (e.g. limestone changes to marble).

3. The rocks of the earth's crust vary in their ability to resist the processes of weathering and erosion.
4. Different rock types produce distinctive landforms.
5. The earth's crust is not a continuous unbroken shell, but rather a number of plates.

## 3.2 The theory of plate tectonics

**(a) The History of Plate Movement**

1. The plates which form the crust of the earth have not always been in their present position, but have moved over millions of years.
2. 200 million years ago the continents that exist today were grouped together to form a single land mass, called Pangea.

## (b) Plate Movement

1. The plates which make up the earth's crust move at an average rate of a few millimetres per year. The movement is caused by **magma** (molten rock beneath the earth's surface) being brought to and taken away from the surface by **convection currents**.

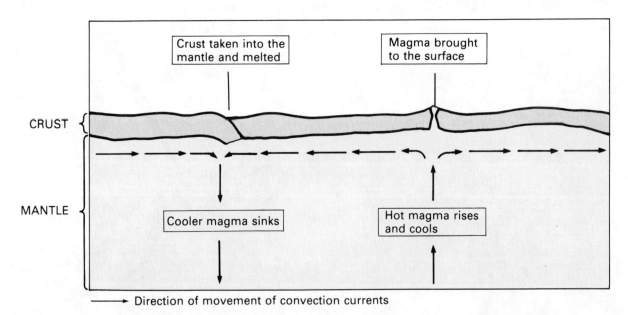

Figure 3.3   Convection currents

2. The magma is forced between two plates on to the surface as **lava** (molten rock on the earth's surface). The lava solidifies and forces the two plates to move apart. Where this process is happening the plate boundary is called a **constructive plate boundary**.
3. As new crust is formed at constructive plate boundaries other crust is destroyed at **destructive plate boundaries**. Here one plate is forced under another in a **subduction zone** and destroyed in the mantle.
4. Sometimes the plates slide and jolt past each other so crust is neither created nor destroyed.

## (c) The Unstable Earth

1. The plate boundaries are lines of weakness along which magma from the mantle can reach the surface.
2. The tremendous forces involved in the creation and destruction of the crust's plates causes a set of processes and landforms to be present.
3. Fig. 3.4 shows the close relationship between the location of the boundaries of the crust's plates and the location of volcanoes, earthquakes and young fold mountains.
4. Because the plate boundaries have moved over a length of time there is evidence that volcanoes, earthquakes, folding and faulting have occurred in areas away from the plate boundaries of today.

15

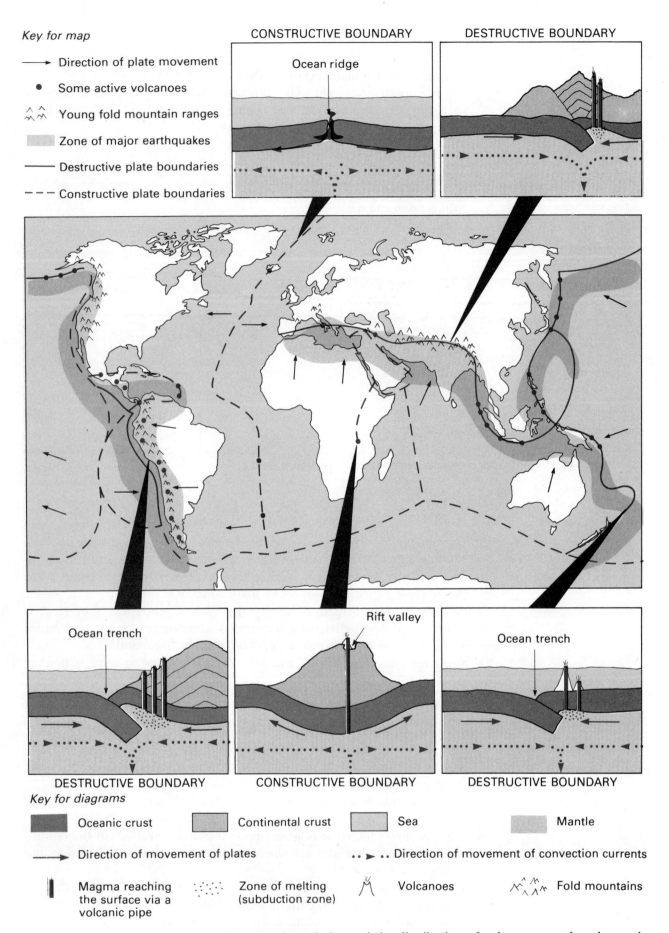

**Figure 3.4** The plate boundaries and the distribution of volcanoes, earthquakes and young fold mountains

# 3.3 Folding and faulting

### (a) Causes and Location of Folding and Faulting

1. On the plate boundaries the rocks of the earth's crust are put under pressure as the plates move against each other.
2. This can cause the rocks to be either folded or cracked (faulted).

### (b) Types of Fold and Fault

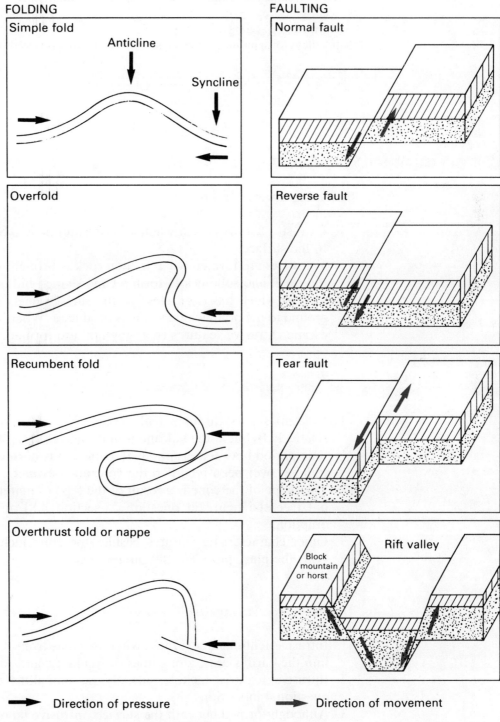

Figure 3.5 Types of fold and fault

## (c) Some Effects of Folding and Faulting

**Table 3.1**  Some effects of folding and faulting

| Positive effects | Negative effects |
|---|---|
| 1. Mountainous regions provide sites for HEP. | Mountains are a barrier to transport. |
| 2. Source area for the water of the world's major rivers. | The climatic conditions associated with mountains limit the agricultural potential. |
| 3. Rift valleys and mountains form interesting landscapes where specialist leisure activities are performed (e.g. skiing). | Mining operations are hampered by folds and faults in the mineral seams. |
| 4. Rift valleys form natural routeways. | Construction needs to take account of fault zones. |

# 3.4  Vulcanicity, the formation of extrusive and intrusive features

### (a) The Formation of Extrusive Features

1. Extrusive features occur when lava or water heated by magma is brought to the surface.
2. **Volcanoes** are formed when molten rock is brought on to the surface of the earth and solidifies to form a cone-shaped hill.
3. Magma which has risen close to the surface heats water stored in the ground to the point where steam is produced. Where this steam is able to escape extrusive features (e.g. geysers) are formed.

### (b) The Characteristics of Volcanoes

1. Volcanoes pass through a life cycle. When eruptions begin and are relatively frequent the volcano is in its **active** stage. When there is a long time period between eruptions the volcano is **dormant**. When no eruption has ever been recorded the volcano is **extinct**.
2. The shape of the cone is a result of the type of material which is thrown out (see the figure in question 2, section 3.8) and the force of the eruption.
3. Other characteristic features besides the cone include the **crater**, the **vent**, the **plug**, **pipes** and **subsidiary cones**.

### (c) The Formation of Intrusive Features

1. Intrusive features are formed when magma, from the mantle, is forced into the earth's crust along lines of weakness and solidifies.
2. Intrusive features include **sills**, **dykes**, **batholiths** and **laccoliths** (see question 4 in section 3.8).
3. Although formed beneath the surface, intrusive landforms may become partly visible on the surface as the rocks above are worn away.

## 3.5  Earthquakes

### (a) The Cause of Earthquakes

1. Earthquakes usually occur at destructive plate boundaries or where one plate is sliding past another.
2. The plates do not always move smoothly under or past each other. Instead, intense pressure builds up until a fracture occurs causing movement to take place in a series of sudden jolts. The shock waves that result from these jolts are called earthquakes.

### (b) The Form of Earthquakes

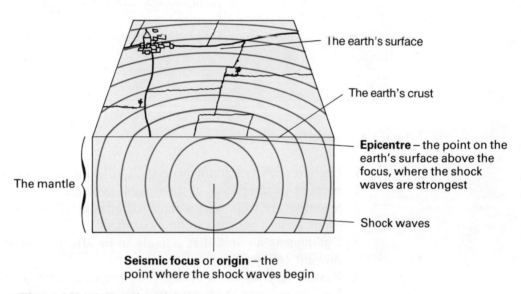

Figure 3.6  An earthquake

### (c) Measuring Earthquakes

1. The force of the shock waves is measured with a **seismometer**.
2. The readings are interpreted by using the **Richter scale**. The scale ranges from 0 to over 8, a high value on the scale representing a strong earthquake.
3. The **Mercalli scale** uses the different effects felt and observed by people to judge the intensity of an earthquake. The scale ranges from 0 to 12, a high value on the scale representing a strong earthquake.

## 3.6  The effect on people of earthquakes and volcanoes

### (a) Positive Effects of Volcanoes

Table 3.2  Positive effects of volcanoes

1. Geysers supply hot water. Volcanic areas are a source of geothermal power.
2. Precious gems, copper, nickel and sulphur can be found in volcanic areas.
3. Volcanoes, baccoliths, laccoliths and geysers form interesting features of the landscape.
4. Lava can weather to form fertile soils.

### (b) Negative Effects of Volcanoes and Earthquakes

1. The lava, ash, **tsunamis** (tidal waves) and the flooding that results, mud slides and fire are the main negative effects associated with a volcanic eruption.
2. The shock waves, tsunamis and the flooding that results, mud slides and fire are the main negative effects associated with an earthquake.

**Table 3.3** Negative effects of volcanoes and earthquakes

| Effect on | Result |
| --- | --- |
| Settlements and services | Communications, gas, water, electricity disrupted. Buildings damaged and destroyed. |
| Agriculture | Crops destroyed and land may be temporarily or permanently out of use. |
| Human life | Life may be lost and people injured. |

### (c) Lessening the Effects

1. Human activity cannot prevent a volcanic eruption or an earthquake because of the power of the forces involved.
2. Scientists try to predict when earthquakes will occur and volcanoes will erupt so that people can be evacuated.
3. Buildings in an area that is likely to be affected can be strengthened to prevent collapse.
4. Rescue services can be prepared to react quickly to the eruption.
5. Lava flows can be prevented from reaching settlements by using explosives to create a channel to divert them, or by encouraging them to solidify by spraying them with water.
6. All these ways of lessening the effects require scientific knowledge and money. Generally the developing countries of the world have fewer resources to lessen the effects.

## 3.7 Structure of the earth examples

**Table 3.4** Structure of the earth examples

| Named examples of | Factual information needed | Your named example |
| --- | --- | --- |
| 1. Constructive and destructive plate boundaries | Name and location of plates. Description of processes operating. Names of associated features (e.g. fold mountains, trenches etc.) | 1.(a) <br> 1.(b) |
| 2. Rift valley <br><br> 3. Fold mountain range | Location and description of the processes operating and the effect that the landforms have on people (e.g. transport, | 2. <br><br> 3. |

| 4. Block mountain | agriculture, water storage etc.) | 4. |
| 5. Volcanic eruption | Location and description of the event, its causes and effects on people and any attempts to lessen the effects. | 5. |
| 6. Earthquake | | 6. |
| 7. Intrusive feature | Location, description of its formation and its effect on people. | 7. |

# 3.8 Questions and answers

## (a) Multiple-choice and Completion Questions

**1** Match the descriptions below with the correct diagrams.

**A** Basic lava volcano. The lava has a high iron content so it has a low melting point and therefore flows further along the surface before it cools and solidifies.

**B** Acid lava volcano. The lava has a high silica content so it has a high melting point and therefore flows only a short distance along the surface before it cools and solidifies.

**C** Composite volcano. The cone is made up of alternate layers of ash and lava. The layers are formed either by an eruption of ash followed by one of lava or by the same eruption where ash and lava settle at different times.

**D** Caldera. The shape of a volcano can be altered by later eruptions. Sometimes the volcanic plug in the vent of the volcano does not move as the pressure builds up from the magma trying to reach the surface. The pressure is so great that part of the top of the volcano is blown off. The top of the volcano may also sink into the mantle below. A lake is sometimes formed.

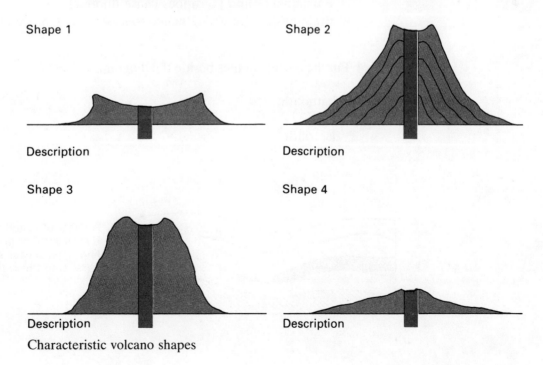

Shape 1

Description

Shape 2

Description

Shape 3

Description

Shape 4

Description

Characteristic volcano shapes

**2** Which of the following is **not** happening in the diagram?

  **A** One plate is being forced under another.
  **B** An ocean trench is being formed.
  **C** Convection currents are moving towards the earth's centre beneath the zone where the two plates are meeting.
  **D** Folding of the crust is taking place.
  **E** Crust is being created.

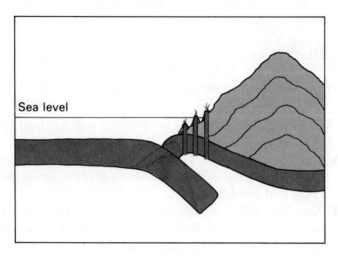

A plate boundary

**3** Which of the following statements about the effect of earthquakes and volcanoes on people is false?

  **A** Water heated below the earth's surface can be used as a power source.
  **B** The prediction of volcanic eruptions prevents them from happening.
  **C** Lava can provide fertile soil for agriculture.
  **D** Earthquakes and volcanoes cause flooding.
  **E** Buildings can be strengthened to lessen the damage of an earthquake.

**4** Put the correct names beside the diagrams below:

  batholith
  dyke
  laccolith
  sill

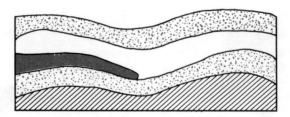

1. A sheet of solidified magma along a horizontal or gently sloping line of weakness which runs parallel to the crust's rocks

Name

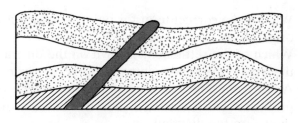

**2.** A sheet of solidified magma along a vertical or near vertical line of weakness which cuts across the layers of the crust's rocks

Name

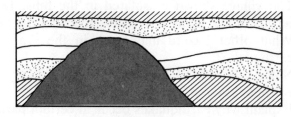

**3.** A large mass of solidified magma which is dome shaped

Name

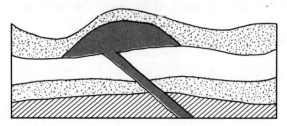

**4.** A mass of solidified magma which is often fed by a dyke and causes the ground above to bulge

Name

Intrusive landforms

**(b) Structured Questions**

**Example 3.1**

(a) Study the diagram below:

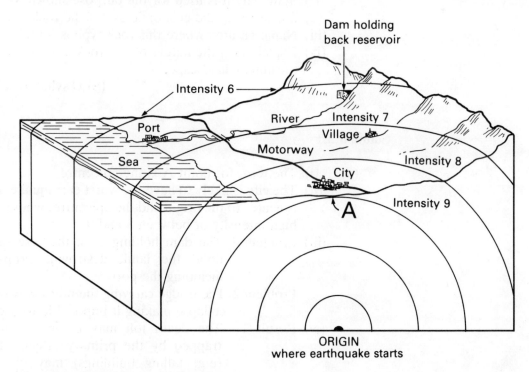

An area affected by an earthquake

(i) What is the correct term for point A, which is directly above the origin of the earthquake?

(ii) Which of the settlements shown on the diagram is likely to have the worst earthquake damage? Give a reason for your answer.

(iii) Apart from direct damage to the settlements, suggest two other problems which could be caused by the earthquake in the area shown on the diagram.

(iv) The village shown is isolated in the hills. Describe two likely results of any delay in rescuers reaching the village.

(v) What other hazard may form in the sea as a result of this earthquake?

(vi) Name one part of the world which is likely to be affected by earthquakes.

(vii) Explain why earthquakes occur in certain parts of the world.

(viii) What scale is used to measure the intensity of an earthquake?

(b) Complete the following table showing information on rock types:

Information on rock types

| Rock type | Example | Economic use |
|---|---|---|
| | Granite | Roadstone |
| Sedimentary | | |
| Metamorphic | | Roofing material |

(c) Write down the name of one of the examples of rocks from your table.
   (i) State why it is used for the purpose shown.
   (ii) Suggest why the economic use of the rock may be limited.
   (iii) Name an area where this rock type is found.
   (iv) Explain how the nature of this rock affects both the physical and the human landscape.

(SEG syllabus A2 question 5 1988)

**Solution 3.1**

(a)   (i) The term for point A is the epicentre.

    (ii) The city is likely to have the worst earthquake damage because it is nearer to the origin and the epicentre, where the quakes have a high intensity of between 8 and 9.

   (iii) Problem 1  The dam holding back the resevoir may burst and flood the land, destroying crops and buildings, including the port.

              Problem 2  The bridge carrying the motorway over the river may collapse making it impossible to use.

   (iv) Result 1   The death toll may be increased because people trapped by the primary effects of the earthquake (e.g. falling buildings) may die before they are rescued.

Result 2     Food and medical supplies will be delayed, increasing the risk of death to those who have survived the primary effects of the earthquake.

(v) A tidal wave or tsunami may form in the sea.

(vi) The west coast of South America.

(vii) Earthquakes occur only in certain parts of the world because the factors which cause them are found only in some areas. Earthquakes are the result of sudden movements in the earth's crust as the plates which make up the crust move against each other. Plates meet and move against each other only in certain parts of the world.

(viii) The Mercalli scale is used to measure the intensity of an earthquake.

(b) See the table below:

Information on rock types

| Rock type | Example | Economic use |
|---|---|---|
| Igneous | Granite | Roadstone |
| Sedimentary | Limestone | Ornamental Garden Stones. |
| Metamorphic | Slate. | Roofing material |

(c) Name of rock from completed table – limestone.

(i) It is used in the garden because the size, colour and shape of individual rocks are attractive.

(ii) The economic use of limestone as ornamental stone is limited because of the high cost of transporting it to non-limestone areas.

(iii) Chapel-Le-Dale in North Yorkshire.

(iv) The nature of limestone creates a distinctive set of landforms that characterise the physical landscape. Surface drainage is limited, dolines and sink holes occur where the process of carbonation has widened the joints and bedding planes in the rock. Dry valleys, eroded before the water found a way underground, can also be found. Steep cliffs or scars can form as limestone is a hard rock. Plateau surfaces are common because the rock was formed as a level bed beneath the sea and erosion has been even.

The white rock is often exposed, sometimes as a limestone pavement, because the process of carbonation does not leave enough material to form more than a thin soil covering.

The human landscape is partly the result of the nature of this distinctive physical landscape. Limestone is used as a resource for building material for walls and houses, and quarries can form part of the human landscape. The limited water supply on the limestone means that settlement tends to be sparse and sited on the spring line where the limestone rests on an impermeable layer. The thin soils favour only sheep-farming.

**Example 3.2**

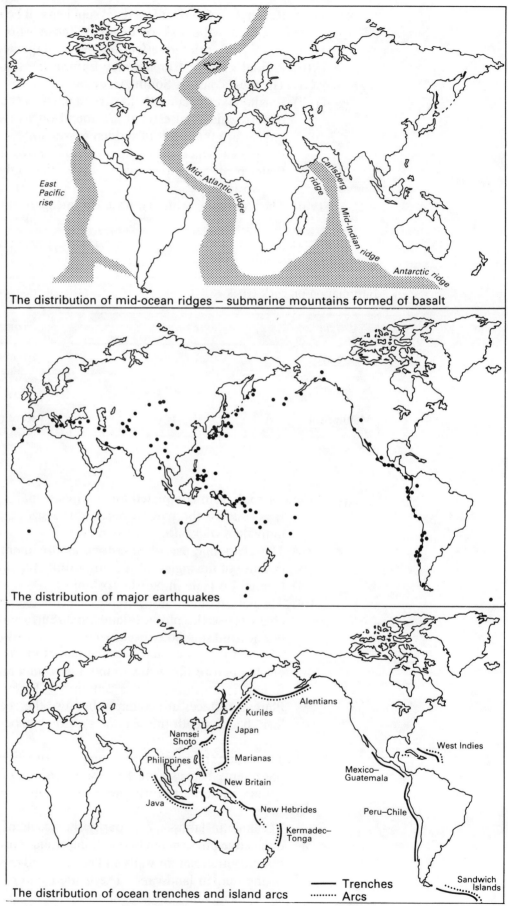

The distribution of mid-ocean ridges – submarine mountains formed of basalt

The distribution of major earthquakes

The distribution of ocean trenches and island arcs

Three world maps showing some major features of the earth –
mid-ocean ridges, ocean trenches, island arcs and earthquakes

(a) Describe the pattern of the features shown by two of the maps opposite.

(b) Explain the pattern shown on one of the above maps.

(c) Name an area which you have studied where the landforms have been influenced by earth movements or volcanic activity. Describe the landforms which have been produced.

(d) Why, in spite of the dangers, do people continue to live in areas threatened by earthquakes and volcanic action?

(**MEG** syllabus D paper 2 question 10 1988)

**Solution 3.2**

(a) **Earthquakes**

The distribution of earthquakes is concentrated in two main areas, around the edge of the Pacific Ocean and in a horizontal belt stretching from the Mediterranean Sea eastwards through Turkey, Iran and Afghanistan to the Himalayas. Within these areas the pattern is clustered.

**Mid-ocean ridges**

The ridges run for most of their length in a north to south direction down the middle of the Atlantic Ocean, from Mexico in the east Pacific Ocean and from the coast of Oman in the Indian Ocean. The latter divides off the island of Madagascar to form two separate ridges, one running in a south-easterly direction to join the mid-Atlantic ridge and the other running in a south-westerly direction becoming the Antarctic ridge.

(b) **Mid-ocean ridges**

Mid-ocean ridges follow the pattern described in (a) because they are formed at constructive plate boundaries. Here magma is brought to the surface by convection currents in the mantle of the earth. The magma is forced between plates and solidifies to create new crust in the form of a basalt ridge.

(c) The Rhine rift valley to the north of Basle is an area where a rift valley has been produced as a result of earth movements. The rift valley consists of a flat-bottomed valley approximately 30 kilometres wide along which the river Rhine flows. The valley sides are steep and consist of a series of steps created by faulting and the horsts of the Vosges and Black Forest Mountains which have been uplifted to a height of between 1000 and 1500 metres above sea level.

(d) People continue to live in areas threatened by earthquakes and volcanoes because they want to use the resources the areas offer (e.g. fertile volcanic soils).

The areas may have been occupied before the threat was known and to leave the area would mean considerable loss of money for individuals and governments. If people were to move they would then have the problem of finding somewhere else to live.

In some areas people may continue to live with the threat because of the preventive measures that are and have been taken. Examples include the attempted prediction of the next event, and in the case of earthquakes pressure release and reinforced buildings.

Finally, people may not perceive the threat accurately, and so continue to live in the area. For example the date of the last earthquake or eruption may not have been in living memory, so the threat may be perceived as non-existent.

**(c) Answers to Multiple-choice and Completion Questions**

**1** **1 D**
   **2 C**
   **3 B**
   **4 A**
**2 E**
**3 B**
**4** **1** sill
   **2** dyke
   **3** batholith
   **4** laccolith

# 4 Weather, Climate and Ecosystems

## 4.1 The elements of weather

### (a) The Elements of Weather and their Measurement

1. Weather is the state of the atmosphere over a short period of time.
2. The weather is made up of a number of elements which can be measured.

**Table 4.1** The elements of weather and their measurement

| Element | Measured by | Units |
|---------|-------------|-------|
| Precipitation | Rain gauge | Millimetres |
| Temperature | Maximum and minimum thermometers | °C |
| Humidity | Hygrometer (wet and dry bulb thermometers) | % |
| Atmospheric pressure | Barometer | Millibars |
| Wind direction | Wind vane | Points of compass |
| Wind speed | Anemometer | Kilometres per hour |
| Cloud cover | Visual | Eighths |
| Hours of sunshine | Sunshine recorder | Hours |
| Visibility | Visual | Metres |

3. The elements are related: a change in one will cause changes in others. Day-to-day variations in the weather are the result of these changes.
4. Weather information from a number of recording stations is shown on a weather map using various symbols.

### (b) The Element of Humidity

1. Humidity is the amount of water vapour in the air. Saturated air has a humidity of 100%.
2. Warmer air can contain more water vapour.

### (c) The Element of Visibility

1. Clouds, fog and mist reduce visibility.
2. They occur when water vapour in the air is cooled to the **dew point** where it **condenses** into tiny droplets of water.

### (d) The Element of Precipitation

1. Precipitation is the deposition of moisture on the earth's surface (rain, hail, snow and sleet).
2. It is formed when air is forced to rise and condense, creating clouds of tiny droplets of water. The droplets join together and will fall when they have become large enough to overcome the updraughts that keep them airborne.
3. Air is forced to rise when two air masses meet at a front (**frontal precipitation**); when it meets a relief barrier (**relief or orographic precipitation**); and when the heat of the sun warms the earth's surface which in turn heats the air near the surface causing it to expand and rise (**convectional precipitation**).

### (e) The Element of Pressure

1. Atmospheric pressure is the weight of a column of air above a point on the earth's surface.
2. Atmospheric pressure falls as altitude increases and when air is forced to rise and expand as the ground surface gives off heat. When air is sinking to the ground the pressure rises.

### (f) The Element of Wind

1. Winds blow from areas of high pressure to areas of low pressure.
2. A large **pressure gradient** (the rate of change in pressure between two areas) will cause stronger winds.

### (g) The Elements of Temperature and Sunshine

1. Radiation from the sun provides heat on the earth. Not all the radiation from the sun reaches the surface of the earth; some is absorbed by the atmosphere and some is reflected.
2. Day-to-day variations in the temperature of a place result from changes in the cloud cover and the nature of the wind.

## 4.2  Weather patterns

### (a) Depressions

1. **Depressions** are areas of low pressure caused by the upward spiral of air at the boundary (**front**) of two different bodies of air (**air masses**).

2. At the polar front a wave is often formed when the warm and moist tropical maritime air mass bulges into the drier and colder polar continental air mass. Two fronts develop, one warm and one cold.

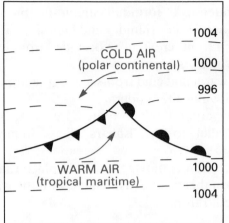

**Stage 1**
Tropical maritime air bulges into the polar maritime air forming a wave in the polar front

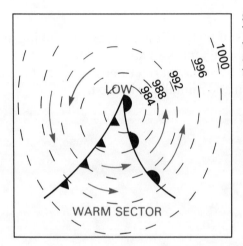

**Stage 2**
The cold front moves faster than the warm front. Pressure falls and isobars and winds form a circular pattern around the area of low pressure

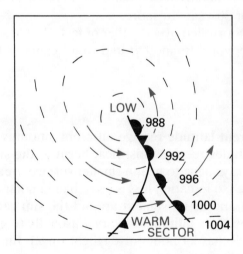

**Stage 3**
The cold front catches up with a section of the warm front reducing the size of the warm sector. Pressure increases and the depression begins to disappear

*Key*

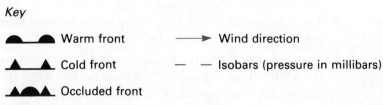

**Figure 4.1** The development of a depression

3. At the warm front the lighter, warm and moist air rises gently over the colder, drier air and condenses to form clouds which release drizzle.
4. At the cold front the denser, colder and drier air forces a wedge underneath the lighter, warmer and moister air causing it to rise quickly. As it rises it condenses to form tall cumulo-nimbus clouds which release heavy rain, and sometimes thunder and lightning. The cold front catches up with the warm front, creating an occluded front where the differences between the air masses are removed.
5. In between the warm and cold fronts a warm sector develops where light drizzle falls and winds are moderate.
6. The winds blow around the low pressure area, at the centre of the depression, parallel to the **isobars** (lines joining places of equal pressure).
7. The whole depression is moving and so a place that it passes over will experience in turn the weather associated with the warm front, the warm sector and the cold front.

### (b) Anticyclones

1. These are areas of high pressure caused by sinking air. Winds are gentle as the pressure gradient is small.
2. The sinking air becomes warmer and is able to take up water vapour so cloud formation and rainfall are limited.

## 4.3  Climatic factors

### (a) Variations in Climate

1. Climate is the generalised summary of weather conditions calculated from records of 30 years or more.
2. The climate is controlled by a number of factors. These factors vary from one part of the world to another and cause climates to vary as well.

### (b) Latitude

1. Places of different latitude receive different amounts of heat annually.
2. Equatorial latitudes receive most heat because the sun is higher in the sky. The sun's rays have to heat a smaller surface area and pass through less atmosphere (so radiation loss is less) than in polar and mid latitudes.
3. The earth's tilt and its movement around the sun cause the amount of heat received by some latitudes to vary seasonally (e.g. the area north of the Arctic Circle has 24 hours of daylight on 21 June and 24 hours of darkness on 22 December).
4. The differences in the heat received by various latitudes create a world pattern of pressure and wind movement.
5. Winds do not blow in a north–south direction because of the rotation of the earth. Standing with your back to the wind in the northern hemisphere the winds are deflected to the right, in the southern hemisphere to the left.

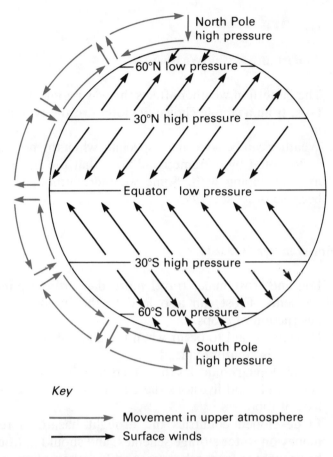

Key

→ Movement in upper atmosphere
→ Surface winds

**Figure 4.2** The world pattern of pressure and wind

**(c) Altitude**

As altitude increases the air becomes thinner and less able to absorb and retain heat, so temperature decreases as altitude increases.

**(d) Distance from the Sea**

1. Water takes longer to heat up and cool down than land.
2. Land near the sea has a smaller **annual range** of temperature (the difference between the highest and lowest temperature) as winds from the sea warm the land in winter and cool it in summer. Areas inland experience **continentality** (extreme temperatures and a large temperature range).
3. Winds blowing from the sea often lose their moisture on the land near the sea and are dry further inland.

**(e) Ocean Currents**

1. Winds blowing across cold currents cool and their water vapour condenses. On reaching the land they are cooler and less likely to bring precipitation.
2. Winds passing over a warm current increase in humidity as the sea water is evaporated. On reaching the land they are warmer and more likely to bring precipitation.

33

# 4.4 Weather as a hazard

## (a) The Importance of the Weather

1. The pattern of weather affects the way people live and the decisions they take, from a simple choice of clothes to the type of house that they live in.
2. Weather can be a hazard, especially when the normal pattern of weather is disrupted by extreme conditions that the people of the area are not used to coping with. Some weather, although expected, is a hazard because of its severity.

## (b) Calm Weather Hazards

1. Fog and frost make travel more dangerous by increasing the risk of accidents. Frost can also lead to the break-up of buildings and the destruction of crops.
2. Drought is said to occur when the amount of water usually received by an area is greatly reduced.
3. In developing countries the effects of a drought can be severe: crops fail, and people and livestock die either due to a lack of drinking water or a lack of food.
4. In developed countries the drought hazard is reduced by spending money on water storage schemes, and should a drought occur water can be brought in from other areas and compensation can be paid to farmers for any loss of crops and livestock.
5. In some areas reduced rainfall frequency combined with the removal of vegetation by human intervention and domestic animals has encouraged the process of **desertification** (the expansion of deserts).

## (c) Storm Weather Hazards

**Table 4.2** The effects of storm weather hazards

| Storm | Hazard | Effect | Reducing the hazard |
|---|---|---|---|
| Tropical cyclone | High winds (up to 300 km per hour). High rainfall (150–300 cm per day) and storm surges cause flooding. | Damage to crops, buildings and property. Injury and loss of life. | 1. Prediction of when, where and with what force the cyclone will strike allows people to secure their property and evacuate the area.<br>2. Coastal defences built to stop storm surges moving inland.<br>3. Buildings strengthened to withstand high winds.<br>4. Compensation paid for damage. |
| Tornado | Unpredictable winds (up to 800 km per hour) | Damage to crops, buildings and property. Injury and loss of life. | No action possible. |

1. **Tropical cyclones** (called **hurricanes** in the Caribbean Sea area and **typhoons** in the China Sea area) are severe depressions with a large pressure gradient that cover an area of approximately 150 square kilometres.
2. As the cyclone moves across the sea it creates a **storm surge** or rapid rise in sea level.
3. **Tornadoes** are funnel-shaped spirals of rapidly rising air that have a diameter of 100 to 150 metres at their base.

## 4.5 Ecosystems

### (a) The Characteristics of an Ecosystem

1. An ecosystem is concerned with the living organisms in an area and how they interact with each other and with the non-living environment of the area.
2. Ecosystems exist at a variety of scales, from the natural region to the rock pool.
3. The non-living components are the soil, rock, light, heat and water.
4. The living components can be divided into:

   (a) **Primary producers**: plants that use the sun's energy to change water and carbon dioxide into carbohydrates releasing oxygen as waste.
   (b) **Consumers** that obtain food by eating plants and animals. Consumers include **carnivores** (meat-eaters), **herbivores** (plant-eaters) and **omnivores** (meat- and plant-eaters).
   (c) **Decomposers**: bacteria that decay dead meat and plants.

5. The components of the ecosystem are linked by a flow cycle of energy, nutrients and water.

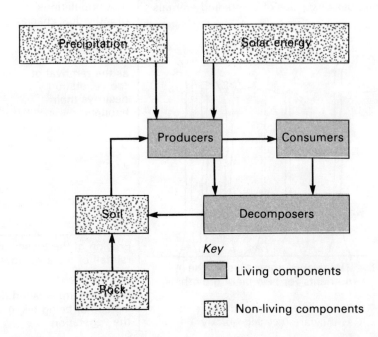

**Figure 4.3** Links between the components of an ecosystem

6. Any of the living components that are not eaten, either while still alive or when dead, by the herbivores or carnivores are broken down by the decomposers and the nutrients from them stored in the soil to be recycled to the vegetation.

7. The links between the consumers are called a **food chain** where the links are simple, and a **food web** where they are more complex.

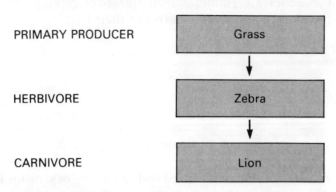

**Figure 4.4** A food chain

### (b) Change within an Ecosystem

1. Gradual change takes place constantly in an ecosystem as the various components adapt to changes in each other. As this process is gradual it does not upset the balance that exists between the components.

2. However, where people have altered a component over a short period of time the balance between the components is upset.

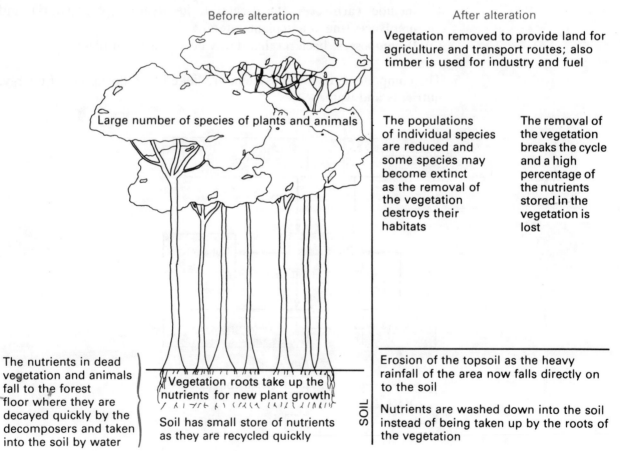

**Figure 4.5** Alterations of an ecosystem by people: the tropical rainforest

## 4.6 Weather, climate and ecosystem examples

**Table 4.3** Weather, climate and ecosystem examples

| Named examples of | Factual information needed | Your named example |
|---|---|---|
| 1. Three contrasting world climates | Name and location. Factors that have caused particular climate. Effects of the climate on people. | 1.(a)<br>1.(b)<br>1.(c) |
| 2. Area that has experienced drought | Name and location of area. Details of drought. Effects of drought on the people and environment of the area. | 2. |
| 3. Tropical cyclone | Name and location of areas affected. Description of the cyclone and its effects. Details of the success or failure of measures to reduce the hazard. | 3. |
| 4. A large-scale ecosystem | Name and location. Description of the system, its use by people and the effects of this use. | 4. |
| 5. A small-scale ecosystem | Name and location. Detailed description of the inputs, outputs, processes and components of the system. | 5. |

## 4.7 Questions and answers

### (a) Structured Questions

**Example 4.1**

(a) Study the graph:

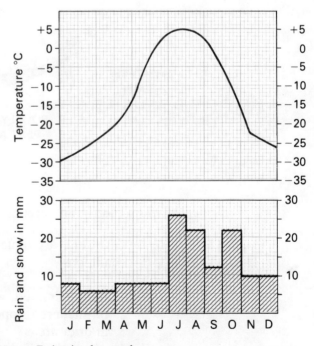

Graph showing the climate of Barrow Point in the tundra

37

(i) Complete the table below:

|  | °C | Month |
|---|---|---|
| Highest temperature |  |  |
| Lowest temperature |  |  |

Temperature at Barrow Point

(ii) How many months is the temperature above freezing?
(iii) The total rainfall is between (tick the correct box in the table below):

|  | 0–50 mm |  | 101–150 mm |
|---|---|---|---|
|  | 51–100 mm |  | 151–200 mm |

Total rainfall at Barrow Point

(iv) Give two problems such a climate is likely to create for people living and working at Barrow Point.

(b) Look at the diagram below:

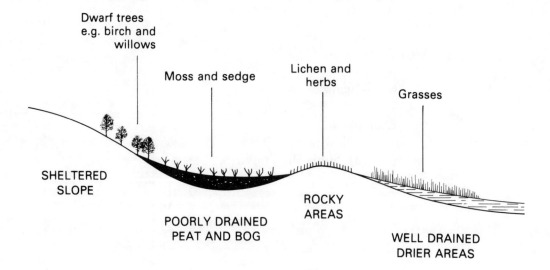

A cross-section of the vegetation in Alaska

Give one example of vegetation which grows in the following conditions:

1. poorly drained, waterlogged soils
2. on sheltered slopes
3. in drier areas
4. where there is little soil

(c) The tundra ecosystem is a very delicate one as the climate is so extreme. Look at the diagram below:

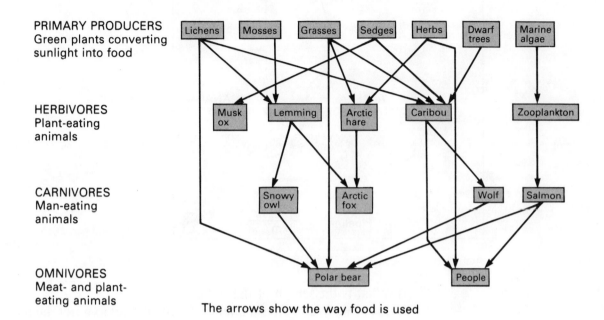

The arrows show the way food is used

The connections between different parts of the ecosystem in the tundra

(i) Complete the table below by giving an example of each of the following:

Examples of different parts of the ecosystem of the tundra

| Primary producer | |
|---|---|
| Herbivore | |
| Carnivore | |
| Omnivore | |

(ii) What food does the lemming depend on?
Food type 1
Food type 2
What food does the arctic fox depend upon?
Food type 1
Food type 2

(iii) What might happen if all the snowy owls were destroyed?
Suggestion 1
Suggestion 2

(d) New oil discoveries were made in Alaska in the 1960s. A pipeline was built to transport the oil from Prudhoe Bay to Valdez. Look at the figure on the next page:

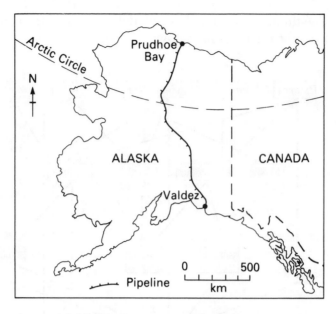

A map of Alaska

(i) What is the length of the pipeline?
(ii) In such a fragile environment it is difficult not to upset the natural ecosystem. Four problems and their solutions are given below, but they are jumbled up. Match the problem and the solution by completing the table. One example has been done for you.

| Problems | Solution | Problem | Solution |
|---|---|---|---|
| 1. Pipeline crosses an active earthquake zone | A Pipeline lifted up to 3 metres above ground | 1. | |
| 2. Large rivers had to be crossed | B Oil heated to 80 °C to keep it flowing | 2. | C |
| 3. Migration of caribou threatened | C Specially insulated underground pipes | 3. | |
| 4. Very cold temperatures | D Vertical and horizontal movement of pipeline occurs without fracturing | 4. | |

Problems and solutions: building a pipeline in the tundra

(e) For any ecosystem you have studied at any scale (not the tundra):
(i) Describe the main features of the ecosystem. (You may draw diagrams to illustrate your answer.)
(ii) Show how the ecosystem has been changed and the effects this has had. (You may draw diagrams to illustrate your answer.)
(iii) How have people reacted to the changes to the ecosystem?

(MEG syllabus E paper 2 question 9 1988)

**Solution 4.1**

(a)  (i) Highest temperature is +5°C in August.
     Lowest temperature is −29°C in January.
   (ii) 4 months.
  (iii) The total rainfall is between 101 and 150 mm.
   (iv) **Problem 1**
     Growing crops to eat will be impossible or expensive so the people will have to rely on hunting or food brought in from outside the area.
     **Problem 2**
     Special precautions will have to be taken to keep warm.

(b)  1. moss
     2. dwarf birch trees
     3. grass
     4. lichen

(c)  (i) See the table below:

| Primary producer | Mosses |
|---|---|
| Herbivore | Lemming |
| Carnivore | Snowy Owl. |
| Omnivore | Polar Bear. |

Examples of different parts of the ecosystem of the tundra

   (ii) The lemming depends on:
     **Food type 1** lichens
     **Food type 2** mosses.

     The arctic fox depends on:
     **Food type 1** lemmings
     **Food type 2** arctic hares.
  (iii) **Suggestion 1**
     The polar bears might have to eat more of their other food sources.
     **Suggestion 2**
     The lemming population might grow unless the arctic foxes can eat the lemmings that the snowy owls used to eat.

(d)  (i) 1300 kilometres
   (ii) See the table below:

(e)  (i) The savanna grasslands are a large-scale ecosystem where the primary producers have adapted to the high input of solar energy, the seasonal input of precipitation and the potentially rapid evapotranspiration. Elephant grass can lie dormant and grow quickly once the rains begin. Most trees have long tap roots to draw up deep water and they lose their leaves in the dry season

| Problems | Solution | Problem | Solution |
|----------|----------|---------|----------|
| 1. Pipeline crosses an active earthquake zone | A Pipeline lifted up to 3 metres above ground | 1. | D |
| 2. Large rivers had to be crossed | B Oil heated to 80°C to keep it flowing | 2. | C |
| 3. Migration of caribou threatened | C Specially insulated underground pipes | 3. | A |
| 4. Very cold temperatures | D Vertical and horizontal movement of pipeline occurs without fracturing | 4. | B. |

Problems and solutions; building a pipeline in the tundra

to reduce transpiration loss. Decomposers act on these and release nutrients for plant growth. The food chain is made up of large herbivores (e.g. wildebeest) who eat the primary producers and are in turn preyed upon by carnivores (e.g. lions) and omnivores (e.g. people).

(ii) Some areas of the savanna ecosystem have been changed by the activities of people. As population pressure has increased, the amount of land used for cultivation and nomadic herding has increased and the fallow period has been reduced.

The reduction in the fallow period and overgrazing have reduced the vegetation cover and exposed the soil to wind and water erosion. The soil, deprived of leaf litter, becomes infertile and unable to support vegetation.

The soil erosion together with the increased area under cultivation has reduced the available habitats of the wild animals. This, together with excessive hunting for food and sport, has reduced the populations of the herbivores and carnivores.

(iii) Where the savanna cannot sustain the population a number of reactions have been observed. Firstly, some farmers have cultivated new areas, temporarily enabling the population to be fed. Secondly, some farmers have adapted their traditional methods of farming, sometimes with help from the government and international oranizations. Adaptations include the introduction of crop rotations and the use of artificial fertiliser and animal manure to maintain the soil fertility. Also irrigation schemes have been used to improve yields. Thirdly, some farmers have migrated either seasonally or permanently to urban centres to try to reduce the population pressure.

People have begun to preserve the wildlife of the savanna by creating game reserves where hunting and the removal of the natural vegetation for agriculture are not permitted. Some endangered species have been bred in captivity to prevent their extinction.

**Example 4.2**

(a) Study the world map below:

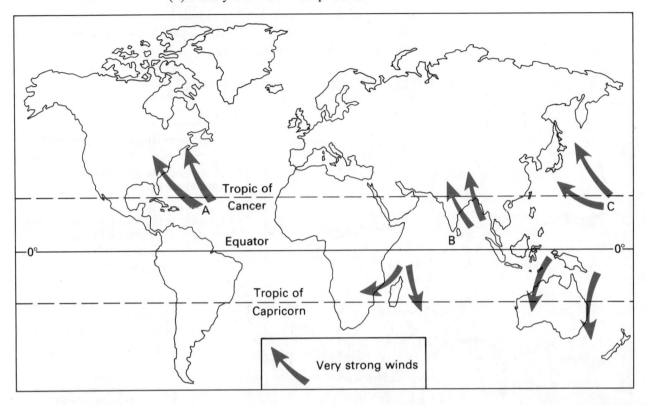

(i) The following are common names for very strong winds: **typhoons**; **hurricanes**; **cyclones**.
Which of these names apply to the winds at A, B, and C on the map?

(ii) State two facts about the origin of most of the world's very strong winds.

(b) Study the diagram below and answer the questions overleaf:

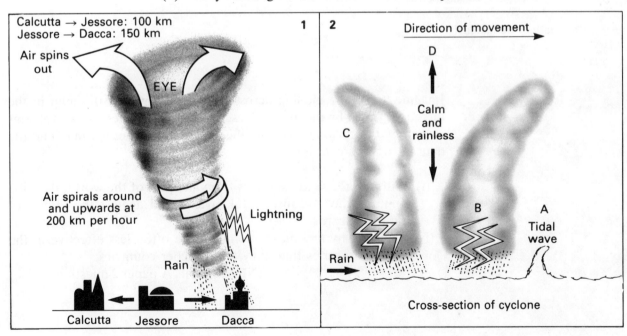

(i) Approximately how far across the top would the cyclone in diagram 1 be? Answer in kilometres.

(ii) Which of the letters (A–D) on the diagram refers to the position of the 'eye' and cumulo-nimbus clouds?

(iii) Describe the sequence of weather conditions you would experience as the cyclone passed over.

(c) Study the map and data in the figure below:

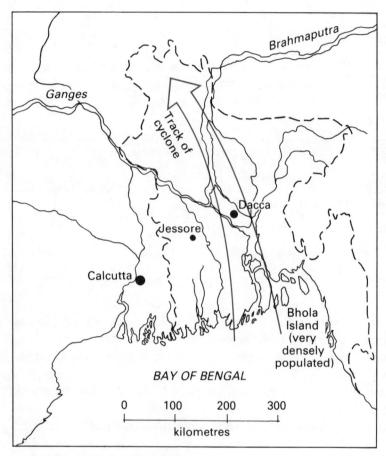

Characteristics of Ganges delta

Average population density: over 200 per sq. km

Main occupation in rural areas: near-subsistence rice farming

Relief: low-lying, swampy

Transport network: poorly developed – lack of major roads or railways

| | Some statistics | |
|---|---|---|
| | *Bangladesh* | *India* |
| GNP per head | 90 US$ | 190 US$ |
| Number of people per doctor | 8780 | 3620 |

— — Boundary of Bangladesh

Imagine a cyclone moving across the area shown on the map in the direction shown by the arrow. Describe the likely effects and problems caused by the cyclone. Use **specific information** from the map and the data to support your answer.

(d)  (i) With reference to examples from any part of the world, describe some of the precautions taken to guard against the effects of natural hazards.

(ii) Explain why any measures taken are often less effective in the poorer countries than they are in richer countries.

(**NEA** syllabus A paper 2 question 5 1988)

**Solution 4.2**

(a)   (i)  A  hurricanes
             B  cyclones
             C  typhoons

     (ii)  Fact 1 – the origin is between the tropic of Cancer and the tropic of Capricorn.
           Fact 2 – the origin is over water.

(b)   (i)  450 kilometres

     (ii)  The 'eye' (D).
           the cumulo-nimbus clouds (C).

   (iii)  The passage of the cyclone can be divided into three stages. First rain, lightning and high winds (up to 200 kilometres per hour) would occur as the cumulo-nimbus clouds pass over. Secondly, there would be a period of calm dry weather as the eye passed over. Thirdly, rain, lightning and high winds would occur again as more cumulo-nimbus clouds passed over.

(c)  The storm surge would flood the area of the map as the land is low-lying. The size of the flooded area would depend on the force of the surge and the exact pattern of relief. Most of the Ganges delta, an area of approximately 60 000 square kilometres, would probably be flooded. Along the track of the cyclone high winds of up to 200 kilometres per hour may occur. The combination of flooding and high winds would damage and/or destroy the rice crop, buildings, the transport network and other services and would cause injury and/or loss of life. The loss of life could be high because of the high population density of 200 per square kilometre; the death toll on Bhola island in particular may be high as it is very densely populated. The destruction of the already poor transport network, the low gross national product per head of Bangladesh (90 US dollars) and India (190 US dollars) and the high number of people per doctor (Bangladesh 8780, India 3620) would combine to increase the death toll as the relief operation would be more difficult.

(d)   (i)  In the USA the prediction of natural hazards such as earthquakes, volcanoes and hurricanes is used as a precaution to reduce the effects. For instance, advanced scientific instruments were used to predict the eruption of Mount St Helena and the people in danger were able to be evacuated.

           In England the Thames Barrier has been built, at a cost of £484 million, to try to protect the city of London from flooding. The barrier is 520 metres long and consists of ten gates that can be closed when a high tide is expected.

     (ii)  The measures taken in poorer countries, both before and after the hazard occurs, are often less effective because the poorer countries do not have as much advanced technology and as much money as the richer countries to pay for the most effective measures. Also, many of the poorer countries lie within the areas where the natural hazards are more severe, so even the best measures would be less effective.

# 5 Shaping the Earth

## 5.1 Earth-shaping processes

### (a) The Process of Weathering

1. **Weathering** is the break-up of rocks that are exposed where they lie.

**Table 5.1** Types of weathering

| | |
|---|---|
| | *Mechanical or physical weathering* |
| Frost shattering | Water enters cracks in the rock and expands as it freezes, causing stresses which eventually break up the rock. The process is more effective in areas where freezing and thawing occur on a daily basis. |
| Temperature change | Heating and cooling cause rocks to expand and contract. This causes stresses which break up the rock because firstly, rock conducts heat badly so the outside of the rock is heated more than the inside and secondly, rock is often made up of different minerals which conduct heat at different rates. |
| | *Chemical weathering* |
| Carbonation | Carbon dioxide in the atmosphere combines with precipitation to form a weak carbonic acid which dissolves the calcium carbonate in rocks such as limestone and chalk. |
| Oxidation | The rock structure is weakened when metallic minerals in rocks combine with oxygen to form oxides. |
| Hydration | Some minerals take up water and expand. The stress that this causes may break up the rock. |
| Hydrolysis | Water combines with some minerals which break down into other forms. |
| | *Biological weathering*<br>*(a combination of physical and chemical weathering)*<br>Rotting plants and animals form acids which help to break down rocks chemically.<br>Plant roots widen cracks in rock physically. |

2. The rate of weathering is dependent on the type of rock, the availability of moisture, the range of temperature and the speed that weathered material is removed to expose new unweathered rock.

### (b) Mass Movement

1. **Mass movement** is the downward movement of material on a slope as a result of gravity.
2. Conditions which promote rapid mass movement include a steep slope angle, an absence of binding vegetation and the availability of sufficient moisture to cause saturation.
3. Rapid mass movement can cause damage to property and loss of life.

**Table 5.2** Types of mass movement

| Type | Description of process |
|------|------------------------|
| Soil creep | The soil particles are moved very slowly downslope, due to gravity when raindrops fall on them, and when they expand and contract due to changes in their temperature. |
| Earth flow | Where the soil becomes saturated it may flow downhill. Where there is a layer of frozen ground beneath on which it can slide the process is known as **solifluction**. |
| Rock falls | Weathering on a steep slope may cause blocks to break off and fall. |
| Landslides | Material on a steep slope may slide downhill in a lump. |

**(c) Erosion**

1. **Erosion** involves the breakdown and removal of material by agents of erosion.
2. The process of erosion is caused by a number of agents:

   (a) running water
   (b) ice
   (c) wind
   (d) waves

# 5.2 Running water, an agent of erosion

**(a) The Movement of Water in the Hydrological Cycle**

The hydrological cycle describes the movement of water on a world scale.

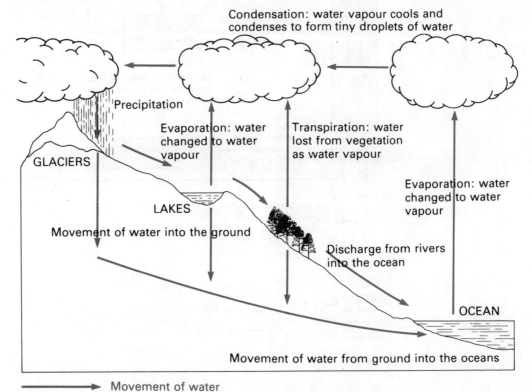

**Figure 5.1** The hydrological cycle

## (b) Movement of Water within the Drainage Basin

1. Individual rivers form a network; the area that a network drains is known as a **drainage basin**. The boundary of the drainage basin is known as the **watershed**.
2. The drainage basin forms part of the hydrological cycle.
3. The drainage basin system shows the inputs, outputs and movement of water within a drainage basin.

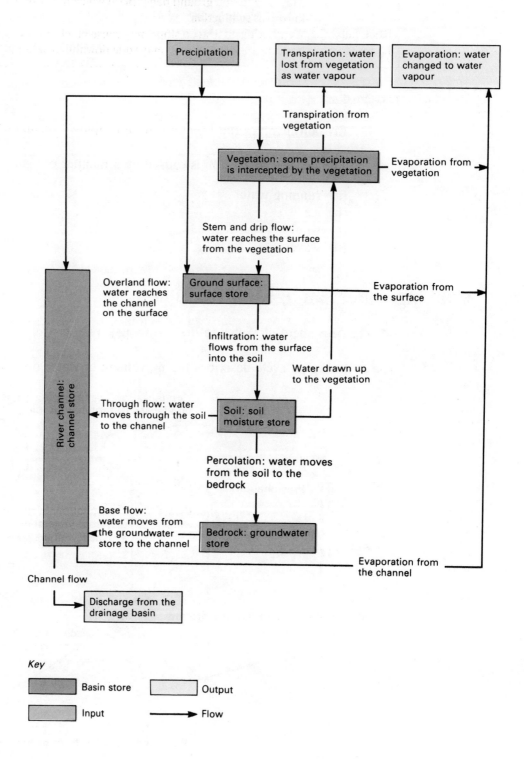

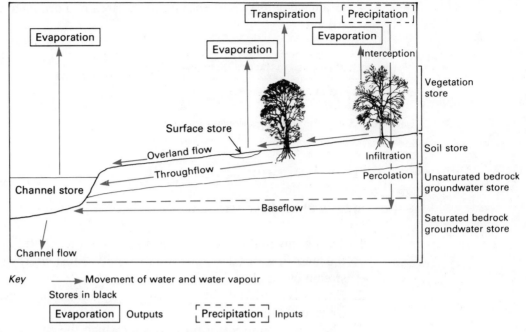

**Figure 5.2** The drainage basin system

## (c) Describing the Drainage Basin

1. The drainage network varies from basin to basin and is described by the technique of stream ordering.
2. Streams flowing from their source are known as first-order streams. When a first-order stream is joined by another first-order stream they form a second-order stream. The joining of two second-order streams creates a third-order stream, and so on.
3. The order of the drainage basin as a whole is that of the highest-order stream.

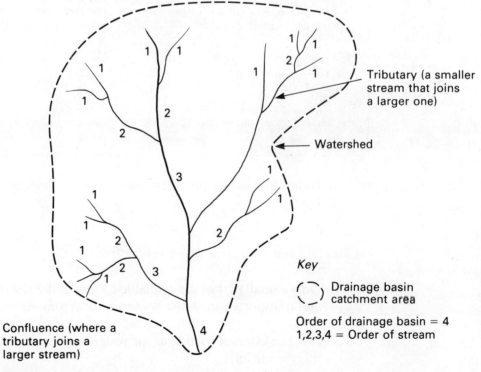

**Figure 5.3** Stream ordering

4. Drainage density is a measure of the area of a drainage basin covered by streams.

$$\frac{\text{Length of streams in the drainage basin}}{\text{Area of drainage basin}} = \text{Drainage density}$$

Figure 5.4   The drainage density equation

## 5.3   Processes in the drainage basin system

### (a) Energy and the Processes in the Drainage Basin System

1. The energy in the drainage basin system is the result of the movement of the mass of water downhill due to gravity. Most energy is available in the stream channel.
2. Energy is needed if the water is to carry out the processes of erosion and transportation.
3. There are a number of processes by which the river erodes its bank and bed and transports its **load** (the material carried by the stream).

Table 5.3   The processes of river erosion and transportation

| Processes of erosion | Processes of transportation |
|---|---|
| **Corrosion** Water dissolves some rocks into solution | **Solution** Dissolved rock is transported in solution |
| **Corrasion** The river hurls its load against its bank and bed | **Suspension** Undissolved light particles are lifted and moved |
| **Hydraulic action** The force of the water as it hits the bed and bank of the river | **Saltation** The river moves bedload downstream in a series of bounces |
| **Attrition** The load itself is eroded as its hits the bank, the bed and itself | **Traction** The river rolls the bedload downstream |
| **Cavitation** Where velocity is high bubbles may form and collapse causing minute shock waves | |

4. Deposition will occur when there is not enough energy to transport the load.

### (b) Friction and Energy in the River System

1. Only a small part of the available energy in the system is used for erosion and transportation. Most is used to overcome two types of friction:

   (a) The **external friction** as the water moves against the bank and bed of the channel,
   (b) The **internal friction** caused by the turbulent flow of the water.

2. The amount of the available energy that is used to overcome friction is controlled by the **efficiency of the channel** (see Fig. 5.5).

*Channel roughness*

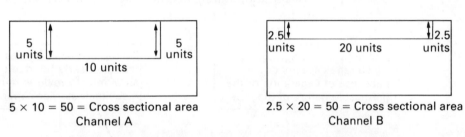

Smooth bed                                    Rough bed

A smooth channel is more efficient than a rough channel because it reduces the cross-sectional area of the channel and cuts down turbulence. Less of the available energy is used to overcome friction

*Channel shape*

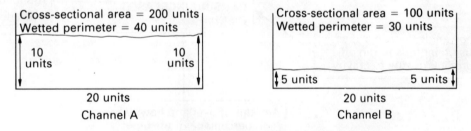

$5 \times 10 = 50$ = Cross sectional area          $2.5 \times 20 = 50$ = Cross sectional area
Channel A                                           Channel B

Channels A and B have the same cross-sectional area but the shape of channel B means that its wetted perimeter (the area of the bank and bed that are under water) is greater. Channel A is more efficient because it uses less of the available energy to overcome external friction

*Water level*

Cross-sectional area = 200 units
Wetted perimeter = 40 units

10 units          10 units

20 units
Channel A

Cross-sectional area = 100 units
Wetted perimeter = 30 units

5 units          5 units

20 units
Channel B

A and B have the same channel shape. A has double the cross-sectional area of B, but its wetted perimeter has only increased by 10 units, Channel A is more efficient. Most channels are more efficient at periods of high flow because a lower percentage of the available energy is used to overcome friction

**Figure 5.5**   Controls on the efficiency of the channel

### (c) Variations in Energy Levels Downstream

1. Energy levels increase downstream as the channel becomes more efficient due to the increases in depth and width, and as the bedload becomes smoother and smaller due to erosion. Less of the available energy is used to overcome friction.
2. Energy levels increase downstream as the discharge (the amount of water passing through a cross-section of the stream in a given time) increases.

3. The discharge increases downstream because:

    (a) The volume of water in the channel increases as the stream drains a larger area.

    (b) The velocity remains constant or increases slightly. (Velocity shows little change because the reduced gradient of the channel is compensated for by the increased channel efficiency). If the velocity decreased the discharge would also decrease.

## 5.4  Variations in energy levels over time

### (a) Variations in Energy Levels

1. The energy that is made available in the stream network by an input of precipitation falling in a drainage basin varies depending on the increase in discharge that results.

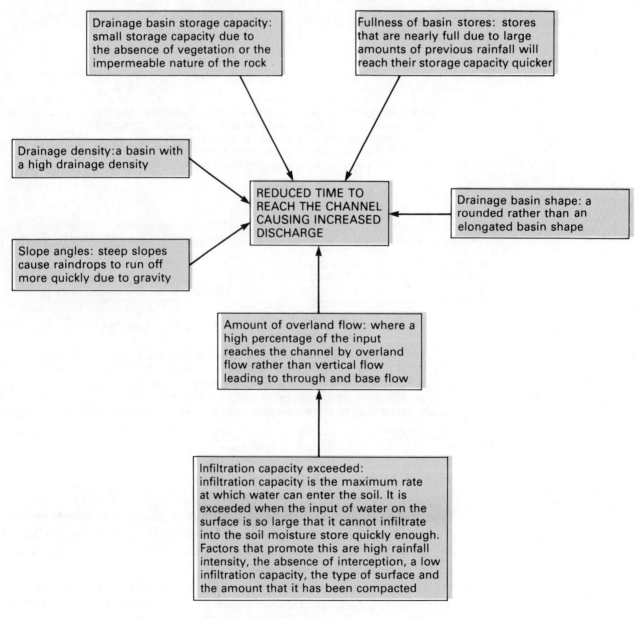

**Figure 5.6**  Factors affecting time taken to reach the channel

52

2. Sometimes the water will reach the channel quickly and at other times slowly. The more quickly the water reaches the channel and the less water that is lost through evapotranspiration, the larger the increase in discharge and therefore energy for the processes of erosion and deposition.
3. The water lost due to evapotranspiration increases when vegetation cover is dense, and interception, surface storage and temperature are high.
4. Within a single drainage basin the drainage density, the shape of the basin and the slope angles are constant over a relatively short period of time. Variations in energy levels are a result of changes in the remaining factors.
5. Energy levels will be different for different basins because all the factors in Fig. 5.6 will vary.

**(b) Describing the Variations**

1. Short-term variations in discharge and therefore energy levels are usually described by a stream or storm **hydrograph**.

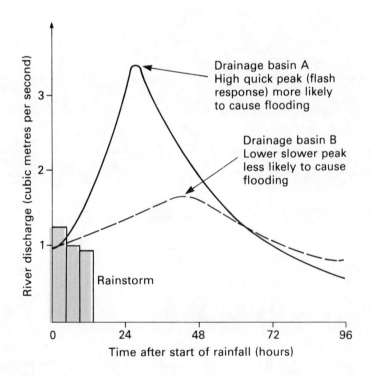

**Figure 5.7**  Stream hydrographs

2. Variations over a longer period of time (usually a year) are referred to as the river's **regime** and shown by a bar chart which plots the volume of water against the months of the year.

## 5.5   The landforms of the river system

### (a)  Features of River Erosion and Deposition

*Interlocking spurs*
These occur where the river is eroding
vertically in a series of bends, a steep-sided
'V' shaped valley which winds around
interlocking spurs

*Waterfalls*
Waterfalls form when the river flows over a
vertical drop (e.g. edge of a plateau or the
side of a deep valley eroded by a glacier).
Alternatively the diagram shows that the
presence of an outcrop of harder rock in the
river channel can lead to the creation of a
vertical drop as the softer rock downstream is
eroded quicker

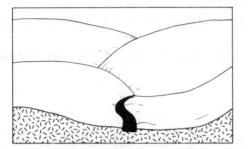

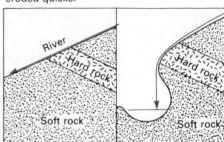

*Floodplain*  As the meanders migrate downstream and laterally (sideways) the
interlocking spurs are eroded to form a wider and flatter valley
floor. When the water exceeds bankfull discharge the valley floor
is flooded and deposition occurs as a result of the increased friction

*Rivercliffs or bluffs*
As the meanders move
downstream and laterally
across the
floodplain the interlocking
spurs are eroded to form
small cliffs

*Terraces*
Where the river
begins to erode vertically
it cuts down into its
floodplain and starts to
create a new floodplain
at the lower level. Parts
of the old floodplain
remain as terraces

*Braiding*
A river may deposit its
load in mid channel due
to a reduction in the
energy available for
transport, forming islands
that the river flows
around

*Levees*
When the bankfull
discharge is exceeded
banks of deposited sedi-
ment may form along the
sides of the river as the
loss of velocity due to increased friction is rapid

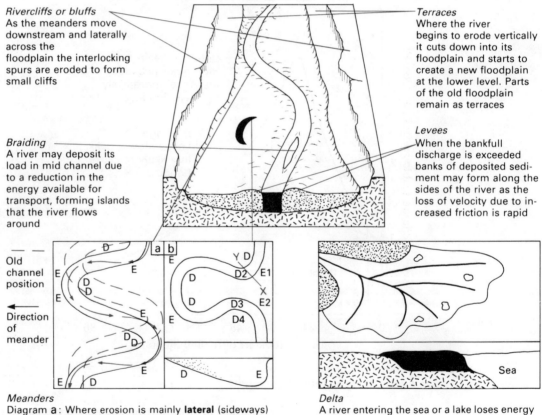

*Meanders*
Diagram **a**: Where erosion is mainly **lateral** (sideways)
the river forms a bend or meander. On the outside of
the bend the water is faster and erosion is taking place
(E points); on the inside deposition occurs (D points).
Meanders move downstream as a result of this pattern
of erosion and deposition eroding the interlocking spurs
to create the floodplain.
Diagram **b**: Sometimes points E1 and E2 meet due to
erosion causing the river to cease to flow around the
bend. The original channel becomes blocked by
deposition at D1, D2, D3 and D4 forming an ox-bow lake
(shaded area)

*Delta*
A river entering the sea or a lake loses energy
and deposits its load, where the load is
allowed to settle and rise above the surface. A
delta is formed

**Figure 5.8**  Features of river erosion and deposition

54

# 5.6 People and the drainage system

### (a) The Drainage System as a Resource for People

1. Water is a vital resource to people for drinking, washing, industrial processes, leisure, agriculture and transport.
2. The landforms that result from river erosion provide ideal locations for a number of human activities:

   (a) Floodplains and terraces in valleys provide fertile areas for agriculture; flat, sheltered land for settlement, industry and transport routes.
   (b) Steep-sided valleys provide sites for the storage of water.

### (b) The Impact of People on the Drainage Basin System

When using the drainage basin people change the inputs, stores, flows and outputs connected with the system. These changes can cause problems for people.

**Table 5.4**  Some examples of people's impact on the drainage basin system

| Use of drainage basin system | Some possible effects on processes | Some possible problems |
| --- | --- | --- |
| Reduction in vegetation, e.g. forest clearance, over-grazing | Reduced evapotranspiration. Increased overland flow. Increased discharge. | Increased flood hazard. Increased soil erosion. |
| Building on land, e.g. settlements, roads | Reduced infiltration. Increased overland flow. | Increased flood hazard. |
| Creation of artificial lake | Increased deposition as river enters lake. Increased erosion by river leaving lake. Peak discharge stored in lake. | Capacity of lake reduced. Reduced flooding means that fertile alluvium does not build up on floodplain. |
| Waste disposal, e.g. industrial effluent and sewage | | Flora and fauna damaged. Drinking water polluted. |

### (c) The Drainage System as a Hazard

1. Flooding is a natural process which can result in the floodplain having fertile soils.
2. Flooding is a hazard because people use and occupy the land near rivers, so floods can cause loss of life and damage to property.
3. Flooding usually occurs as a result of heavy rainfall which causes overland flow and a quick response time. The activities of people in the drainage basin can increase the chance of flooding.

4. The hazard of flooding can be reduced by studying the discharge levels of the past to try to predict the size of the flood and the area that it will cover, and then taking steps to prevent or minimise the damage caused by the flood.

**Table 5.5** Ways of preventing and minimising the flood hazard

1. Enlarge the channel so that it can hold more water.
2. Build embankments on either side of the channel to prevent the spread of flood water.
3. Build extra channels to take flood water away from towns.
4. Build reservoirs near the source of a river to store water and control peak discharge.
5. Prevent building in areas where flooding is most likely.

# 5.7  Shaping the earth examples

**Table 5.6**  Shaping the earth examples

| Named examples of | Factual information needed | Your named example |
|---|---|---|
| 1. Mass movement caused by natural processes with no direct influence by people. | Name of the location and type of mass movement. Description of the processes operating including specific causes. The effect on people. | 1. |
| 2. Mass movement caused partly or wholly by people. | | 2. |
| 3. A flood resulting from natural processes with no direct influence from people. | Name and location of the flood. Description of the processes operating including causes. | 3. |
| 4. A flood caused partly or wholly by people. | The effect on people. | 4. |
| 5. A scheme to reduce the flood hazard. | Name, location and a description of the aim of the scheme and how it affects the processes that are operating. | 5. |
| 6. The use of the drainage by people for agriculture and forestry. | | 6. |
| 7. The use of the drainage basin by people as a means of waste disposal. | Location of the use. Description of the use and its effect on the drainage basin system. | 7. |
| 8. The use of the drainage basin by people for water storage. | | 8. |

| 9. A river regime | Location of river. Description and explanation of the regime. | 9. |
|---|---|---|
| 10. The landforms created by the processes of erosion and deposition. | Name and location of landform. Description of any use by people. | 10. |

# 5.8  Questions and answers

## (a)  Multiple-choice and Completion Questions

1  Which of the conditions listed below is most likely to increase the time that water falling on a particular drainage basin takes to reach the channel?

   A  full basin stores
   B  compaction of the surface
   C  the presence of overland flow
   D  high-intensity rainfall
   E  a high infiltration rate

2  Which of the landforms listed below is formed by the process of deposition?

   A  waterfall
   B  delta
   C  rivercliff (bluff)
   D  interlocking spur
   E  river pothole

3  Which of the weathering processes listed below is a process of mechanical weathering?

   A  carbonation
   B  frost shattering
   C  hydration
   D  hydrolysis
   E  oxidation

4  Which of the statements below does **not** describe a likely effect of building a reservoir in a drainage basin?

   A  The flood hazard is reduced.
   B  The amount of evaporation is increased.
   C  The storage capacity of the basin is reduced.
   D  The reliability of the water supply is increased.
   E  Settlements have to be relocated.

**5** For this question one or more of the responses given are correct. Decide which of the responses is (are) correct. Then choose:

  **A**  if 1, 2 and 3 are all correct
  **B**  if 1 and 2 only are correct
  **C**  if 2 and 3 only are correct
  **D**  if 1 only is correct
  **E**  if 3 only is correct.

Which of the statements below about friction in the river channel are correct?

  1. An increase in the percentage of the available energy that is used to overcome friction causes an increase in the amount of erosion and transportation.
  2. Channel shape affects the amount of external friction.
  3. Internal friction is caused by the turbulent flow of water.

**(b) Structured Questions**

**Example 5.1**

  (a)  Look at the diagram below:

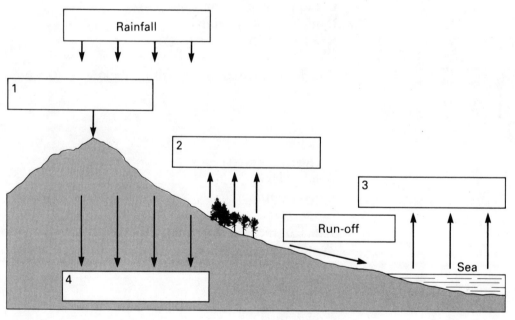

A cross-section of a drainage basin

  (i)  Complete the figure by writing the following words in the correct boxes:
  evaporation
  transpiration
  infiltration
  watershed
  (ii)  What does the term run-off mean?
  (iii)  Describe the movement of water through a drainage basin, starting with the input of water as rainfall.

(b) Look at the table below:

|  | J | F | M | A | M | J | J | A | S | O | N | D |
|---|---|---|---|---|---|---|---|---|---|---|---|---|
| RAINFALL (mm) | 76 | 174 | 71 | 103 | 93 | 95 | 74 | 79 | 71 | 51 | 130 | 331 |
| RUN-OFF (mm) | 93 | 143 | 69 | 84 | 47 | 27 | 12 | 24 | 21 | 30 | 65 | 315 |

Rainfall and run-off totals at a river recording site

(i) Complete the bar graph below to show rainfall and run-off in each month:

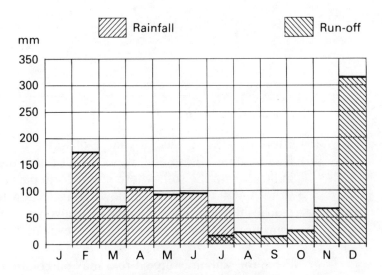

Bar graph to show rainfall and run-off in each month

(ii) Using the bar graph, state how the run-off in winter differs from that in summer.
(iii) Suggest reasons for your answer in (b) (ii).
(iv) Give two factors, other than rainfall, which affect the amount of run-off.

(c) Using the information in the bar graph, suggest why a reservoir might be built in this drainage basin.
(d) Using examples you have studied:
(i) Describe the advantages that some areas have for the building of reservoirs.
(ii) Explain why some people object to plans to build reservoirs.

(**LEAG** syllabus A paper 2 question 5 1988)

**Solution 5.1**

(a)   (i)  See the figure below:

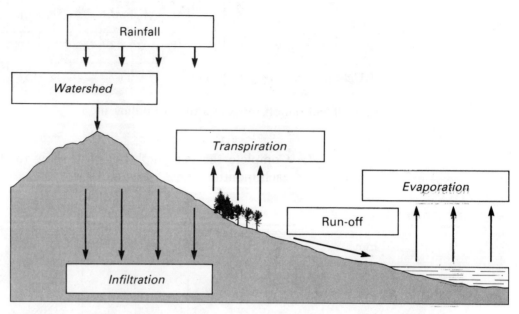

A cross-section of a drainage basin

   (ii)  Run-off is the surface discharge of water.

   (iii) Rain falling within the watershed of the drainage basin may infiltrate into the soil, where it may form part of the soil moisture store and flow as throughflow, contributing to run-off when it reaches the surface. Rain may be drawn up by the vegetation and transpired as water vapour to be recycled.

   From the soil moisture store it may percolate to the groundwater store and flow as base flow.

   Alternatively, on reaching the surface it may flow over the surface as run-off. Any water on the surface may be evaporated into the atmosphere as water vapour to be recycled.

(b)   (i)  See the figure below:

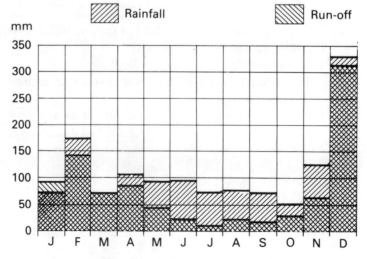

Bar graph to show rainfall and run-off in each month

(ii) Assuming that the figures refer to a river in the Northern Hemisphere and that winter occurs between November and February and summer occurs between May and August the run-off in winter is greater by 516 mm than the run-off in summer. The monthly average for summer is 27.5 mm and for winter 154 mm. The run-off in winter also fluctuates much more than in summer.

(iii) The run-off in winter is greater than the run-off in summer because the rainfall is greater in winter. The run-off in winter fluctuates more than in summer because the rainfall fluctuates more in winter and because some of the water falls as snow in winter and is stored on the surface until it melts.

(iv) **Factor 1**

The amount of evaporation: high evaporation reduces run-off.

**Factor 2**

The amount of transpiration: high transpiration reduces run-off.

(c) The drainage basin has an adequate amount of annual rainfall to maintain a store of water in a reservoir. The drainage basin also has a period between May and October when both rainfall and run-off are low. This might create problems of water supply for the people of the area. A reservoir would increase the supply in these months by storing the water from the heavy rainfall months of November, December and February. Storing the run-off, especially in December, may reduce the risk of flooding.

(d) (i) The area near the headwaters of the North Tyne river in Northumberland was chosen as the site of Kielder Water because of the advantages of the area. The limited agricultural value of the land meant that few people needed to be moved and agricultural resources would not be wasted.

A good site for the dam was found where the foundations were on hard rock and the valley narrowed cutting down the length of the dam. Upstream from the dam the valley widened creating a large storage area. The high rainfall (average monthly rainfall of 100 mm) falling throughout the year and the large catchment area meant that the dam could maintain a high volume of supply.

The area was close to the cities of the North East, cutting down the cost of pipelines to move the water and allowing for leisure developments on and around the reservoir.

(ii) The building of a reservoir often benefits only the people who are using the water, who usually live in the major cities, but does little for the local inhabitants who often object to the plans. The Sobradinho Dam in Brazil caused 70 000 people to be moved from their traditional homes, few jobs to be created as the construction work was capital intensive and fertile agricultural land to be flooded.

Conservationists opposed the development of the Kielder project on the grounds that the reservoir, dam and associated coniferous tree planting had a bad visual impact on an area of natural beauty.

People who wish to use the reservoir for recreational purposes object when access for leisure activity is denied (e.g. Thirlmere).

### (c) Problem-solving Questions

### Example 5.2

#### Part A    The cause of flooding

(a) Study the figure below:

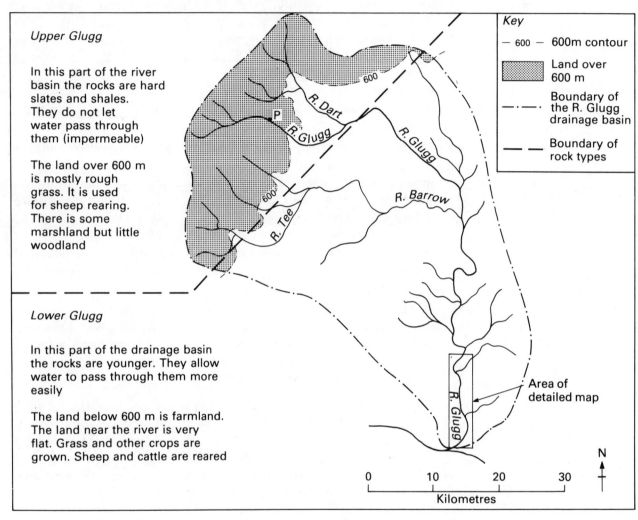

*Upper Glugg*

In this part of the river basin the rocks are hard slates and shales. They do not let water pass through them (impermeable)

The land over 600 m is mostly rough grass. It is used for sheep rearing. There is some marshland but little woodland

*Lower Glugg*

In this part of the drainage basin the rocks are younger. They allow water to pass through them more easily

The land below 600 m is farmland. The land near the river is very flat. Grass and other crops are grown. Sheep and cattle are reared

**Key**

— 600 —  600m contour

Land over 600 m

·—·—·  Boundary of the R. Glugg drainage basin

— —  Boundary of rock types

Area of detailed map

The drainage basin of the River Glugg

(i) Name a tributary of the River Glugg.

(ii) What is meant by the term 'drainage basin'?

(iii) On the map draw in the boundary of the River Barrow's drainage basin.

(iv) What is the boundary line of a drainage basin called? (It is marked ·—·—· on the map.)

(v) From the map give two reasons why heavy rain in the Upper Glugg is likely to cause flooding lower down the drainage basin.

Table showing the monthly rainfall at P in the Upper Glugg valley

| Rainfall in the Upper Glugg valley | J | F | M | A | M | J | J | A | S | O | N | D |
|---|---|---|---|---|---|---|---|---|---|---|---|---|
| Monthly rainfall (mm) | 173 | 128 | 105 | 95 | 95 | 90 | 120 | 138 | 147 | 149 | 180 | 185 |

(vi) Finish the graph below by using the figures in the table above:

62

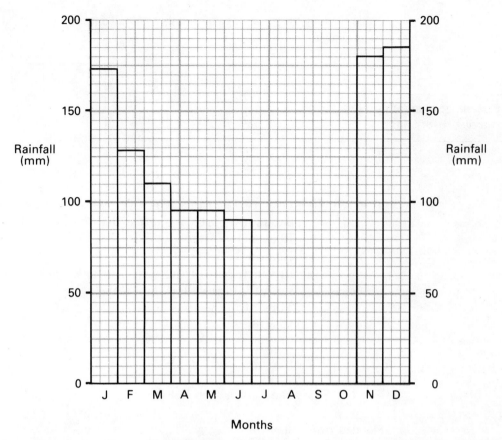

Rainfall in the Upper Glugg valley

(vii) Describe how the rainfall is distributed through the year.

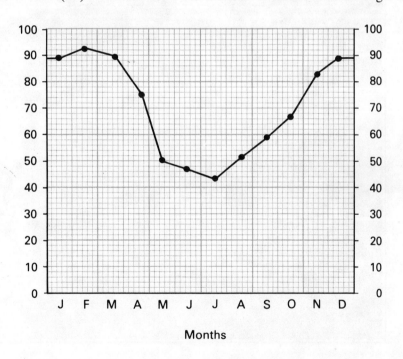

Graph showing the percentage of monthly rainfall entering the
River Glugg

(viii) Use the graph above to complete the table below.

Table showing the percentage of monthly rainfall entering the River Glugg

|  | J | F | M | A | M | J | J | A | S | O | N | D |
|---|---|---|---|---|---|---|---|---|---|---|---|---|
| Percentage of monthly rainfall entering River Glugg | 89 | 93 | 90 | 75 |  |  |  | 52 | 58 | 67 | 83 | 89 |

(ix) Give two reasons why over 90% of the total monthly rainfall enters in February but less than half in June and July.
Reason 1
Reason 2

(x) In which part of the year are floods most likely to occur in the Lower Glugg valley? Say why.
Time of the year
Reason

**Part B    The effects of flooding**

(b) Study the photograph below:

Flooded river valley

(i) Does the floodwater seem to be very deep? YES or NO
(ii) Give a reason for your answer to (b) (i).
(iii) Why does the floodwater not extend even further away from the river?

(c) Study the figure below:

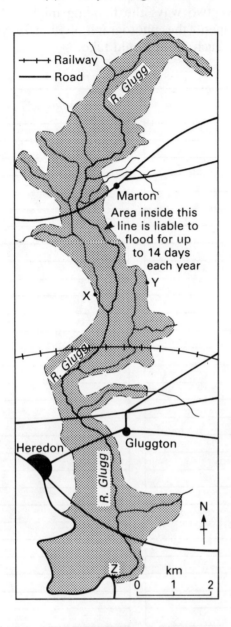

(i) How wide is the flooded area between X and Y?
(ii) Which of the following is the best estimate of the area of flooding?

Tick one of the boxes

| 10 sq km | 25 sq km | 40 sq km | 55 sq km |
|----------|----------|----------|----------|
|          |          |          |          |

(iii) Choose three of the groups in the table below. For each group chosen give two ways the flooding might affect the groups of people named (the photograph may help you). Suggest one precaution each group could take.

| Group | Effects | Precautions |
|---|---|---|
| **FARMERS** | 1. _____ <br><br><br> 2. _____ | |
| **LOCAL RESIDENTS** | 1. _____ <br><br> 2. _____ | |
| **TRANSPORT AUTHORITIES** (in charge of roads and bridges) | 1. _____ <br><br> 2. _____ | |
| **EMERGENCY SERVICES** (e.g. fire brigade, ambulance service) | 1. _____ <br><br> 2. _____ | |

**Part C**

The figure below shows three schemes that have been suggested. Each scheme has advantages and disadvantages. Which should be chosen?

66

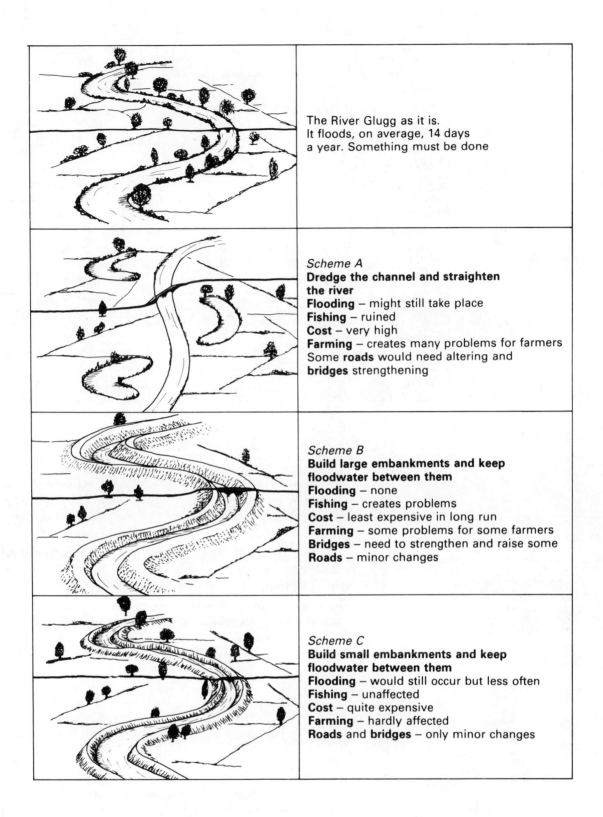

The River Glugg as it is.
It floods, on average, 14 days
a year. Something must be done

*Scheme A*
**Dredge the channel and straighten
the river**
**Flooding** – might still take place
**Fishing** – ruined
**Cost** – very high
**Farming** – creates many problems for farmers
Some **roads** would need altering and
**bridges** strengthening

*Scheme B*
**Build large embankments and keep
floodwater between them**
**Flooding** – none
**Fishing** – creates problems
**Cost** – least expensive in long run
**Farming** – some problems for some farmers
**Bridges** – need to strengthen and raise some
**Roads** – minor changes

*Scheme C*
**Build small embankments and keep
floodwater between them**
**Flooding** – would still occur but less often
**Fishing** – unaffected
**Cost** – quite expensive
**Farming** – hardly affected
**Roads** and **bridges** – only minor changes

(d) (i) For each scheme describe how the scenery is affected
Scheme A
Scheme B
Scheme C

(ii) Complete the table below. For each group of people or organisation give each scheme a score of 3 (best) or 2 or 1 (worst). One row has been done for you. The local people in a house not liable to flood think Scheme C is the best for them (3) and Scheme B is the worst (1).

| Group of people or organisation | Scheme A | Scheme B | Scheme C |
|---|---|---|---|
| Farmers | | | |
| Local people in a house liable to flood | | | |
| Local people in a house not liable to flood | 2 | 1 | 3 |
| Ministry of Transport (in charge of roads and bridges) | | | |
| Water Board (who pay for the scheme) | | | |
| Fishing club | | | |
| Countryside Commission (look at your answer to (c) (i)) | | | |
| TOTAL | | | |

(iii) For the farmers, say why you ranked the scheme in that order.

(iv) Which scheme does the table suggest should be chosen? Say why.
Scheme
Reason

(v) Name one group or organisation for whom this would not be the best scheme. Say why.
Name of group
Why it is not the best scheme

(vi) When deciding on which scheme should be chosen some views carry more weight than others. Which two groups or organisations are likely to have most influence? In each case say why.
Group
Why
Group
Why

(vii) Which group's views do you feel are unimportant? Say why.
Group
Why

(viii) Now put together the information you have gained from Part C. Make a decision on which of the three schemes you would choose.
Explain clearly how you arrived at this decision and why you think this scheme is better than the other two in terms of
1. cost
2. the effect on people's lives and livelihood
3. the environment.
Scheme

(**MEG** syllabus E paper 1 1988)

**Solution 5.2**

**Part A   The cause of flooding**

(a)   (i)  The River Barrow.
  (ii)  The drainage basin is the area drained by a river system.
  (iii)  See the figure below:

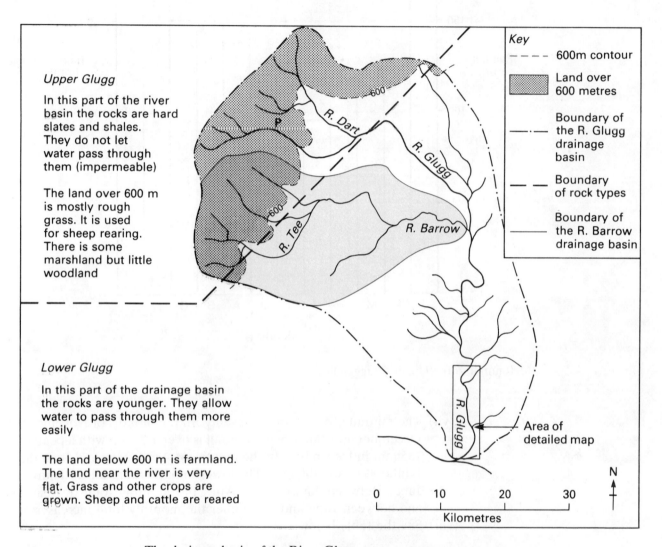

The drainage basin of the River Glugg

  (iv)  The boundary line of the drainage basin is called the watershed.
  (v)  **Reason 1**
  Heavy rain falling in the Upper Glugg cannot percolate into the rock because it is impermeable so more water will reach the rivers by throughflow and overland flow.
  **Reason 2**
  The small amount of woodland in the Upper Glugg will reduce evapotranspiration so more of the rainfall will reach the rivers.

(vi) See the figure below:

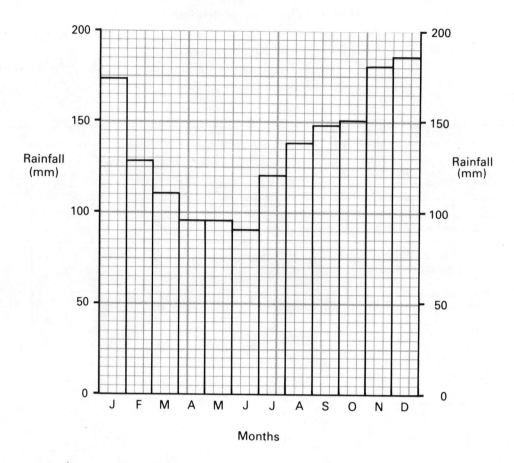

Rainfall in the Upper Glugg valley

(vii) The rainfall is distributed unevenly. In the months of November, December and January the rainfall is over 170 mm with a peak of 185 mm in December. In the months of April, May and June the rainfall is below 100 mm. The lowest monthly rainfall is 90 mm in June. Between January and April the monthly total decreases and between June and November the monthly total increases.

(viii) See the table below:

Table showing the percentage of monthly rainfall entering the River Glugg

|  | J | F | M | A | M | J | J | A | S | O | N | D |
|---|---|---|---|---|---|---|---|---|---|---|---|---|
| Percentage of monthly rainfall entering River Glugg | 89 | 93 | 90 | 75 | 50 | 47 | 43 | 52 | 58 | 67 | 83 | 89 |

(ix) **Reason 1**
In February the stores in the drainage basin are fuller than in June and July so they absorb a lower percentage of the monthly rainfall.

**Reason 2**

In June and July a higher percentage of the monthly rainfall leaves the drainage basin as evapotranspiration than in February.

(x) **Time of year**

January and December.

**Reason**

The Lower Glugg is most likely to flood in January and February because both the monthly rainfall and the percentage of monthly rainfall entering the river are high, so at this time of year the amount of water entering the river is greatest.

**Part B    The effects of flooding**

(b)   (i) No.

(ii) Walls that form the boundary of flooded fields protrude above the floodwater.

(iii) The floodwater does not extend further from the river because at the edge of the floodplain the land increases in height.

(c)   (i) 1.4 km

(ii) 25 sq km

(iii) **Group – farmers**

**Effect 1**

The farmers who own land that has been flooded would not be able to use it until the water had drained away.

**Effect 2**

The load of the river will be deposited on the farmers' land and improve the fertility of the soil.

**Precaution**

At times of heavy rain the farmers could move livestock to higher areas that do not flood.

**Group – local residents**

**Effect 1**

The houses of local residents might become cut off from shops and services.

**Effect 2**

Local residents who want to pursue leisure activities such as fishing in the river and walking along the river would be unable to do so.

**Precaution**

Local residents likely to become cut off could have emergency stores of food and alternative heat and light sources.

**Group – transport authorities**

**Effect 1**

The transport authorities would have to spend time and money repairing any damage that the flooding has caused to the roads and railways.

**Effect 2**

The transport authorities may have to put out warning signs and diversion signs to help road users.

**Precaution**

The transport authorities could prepare a plan so that warnings and diversion signs could be quickly introduced.

(d) (i) **Scheme A**
The scenery is changed considerably: a large number of trees on and away from the river banks would be removed, small lakes would be created and the river would cease to wind over the floodplain.
**Scheme B**
The scenery is changed: a large number of trees growing on the river bank would be removed, the banks would obscure the river and the roads and bridges would become more noticeable.
**Scheme C**
The scenery would be changed slightly: some trees on the river bank would be removed and the banks would slightly obscure the river.

(ii) See the table below:

| Group of people or organisation | Scheme A | Scheme B | Scheme C |
|---|---|---|---|
| Farmers | 1 | 2 | 3 |
| Local people in a house liable to flood | 2 | 3 | 1 |
| Local people in a house not liable to flood | 2 | 1 | 3 |
| Ministry of Transport (in charge of roads and bridges) | 1 | 2 | 3 |
| Water Board (who pay for the scheme) | 1 | 3 | 2 |
| Fishing Club | 1 | 2 | 3 |
| Countryside Commission (look at your answer to (c) (i)) | 1 | 2 | 3 |
| TOTAL | 9 | 15 | 18 |

(iii) I ranked the schemes for the farmers depending on the amount of problems that each scheme would create. Scheme A creates most problems as farm boundaries would change, making it difficult to decide who owns the land. Scheme B, by stopping flooding altogether, would deprive the soil of nutrients deposited by the floodwater so the farmers would have to spend more on artificial fertiliser. Scheme C has the least problems.

(iv) Scheme C should be chosen because it has the highest total, which means it is more popular than the other schemes.

(v) **Group – local people in a house liable to flood**
This is because flooding would still occur if scheme C was introduced, causing damage to the houses of the group. However, under scheme B no flooding will occur so it is more popular than scheme C.

(vi) **Group – the water board**

The views of the water board are very important because they are paying for the scheme and the amount of money that they make available decides which of the alternatives are possible. Also, they are a large organisation with experience at persuading other groups of people to adopt their viewpoint.

**Group – the farmers**

The views of the farmers are important because their standard of living may be affected by the schemes. Also, they may belong to a union that is experienced at protecting the interests of its members.

(vii) **Group – the fishing club**

This group's views are unimportant because their quality of life is hardly affected. The section of the river to be altered is relatively short and therefore they can fish other sections of the river.

(viii) **Scheme C**

I think that the views of the people who live and work in the area are the most important as any changes will alter their lives for a considerable time. Although scheme C is not the cheapest, in financial terms, it causes the least disruption for the local people. I think it is worth the extra cost for this reason.

Scheme C is a good compromise between the need to remove the flood hazard for the local people, whose houses are liable to flood, and the needs of the farmers and local people in houses not liable to flood, who want to minimise the changes to the environment. Scheme C will reduce the flood hazard, but it will cause the least problems for farmers, who will be able to maintain their livelihood, and it will disrupt the quality of life of the local people to the least extent.

Schemes A and B would both involve greater changes to the environment, the roads and bridges, the fishing, the farming, the course of the river, the views of the area and the number of trees. These changes would reduce the livelihood of the farmers and the quality of life of the local residents.

(d) **Answers to Multiple-choice and Completion Questions**

1 E
2 B
3 B
4 C
5 C

# 6 Natural Resources

## 6.1 Types of resources

### (a) Natural Resources

1. **Natural resources** are largely unchanged materials of the land that are of value to people.
2. Natural resources are used by people in a variety of ways.

**Table 6.1** Some natural resources and their uses

| Natural resource | Renewable/ non-renewable | Uses |
| --- | --- | --- |
| Oceans and seas | Renewable | Fish, wave and tidal power, waste disposal site, leisure activities, transport |
| Agricultural land | Renewable | Food and industrial crops and animals |
| Areas of natural beauty | Renewable | Leisure |
| Rivers and lakes | Renewable | Water for homes and industry, waste disposal, leisure, electricity generation |
| Minerals | Non-renewable | Ores for industrial processes, fuels for energy |
| Timber | Renewable | Fuel for energy, timber for building, wood for industrial processes, forests for leisure |

### (b) Renewable and Non-renewable Resources

1. Natural resources can be described as renewable or non-renewable.
2. **Renewable** natural resources can be recycled or re-used. Provided they are managed with care they will not run out.
3. **Non-renewable** or **finite** natural resources occur in limited amounts and if use continues they will run out.

74

**Table 6.2** Energy resources

| Energy resource | Some uses | Other information |
|---|---|---|
| Fossil fuels:<br>Coal | Industrial processes (e.g. steel). Electricity generation. Domestic heating. | Non-renewable. Coal, formed by the decomposition of vegetation to carbon, is mined. Oil and natural gas, formed as tiny micro-organisms decay to hydrocarbons, are drilled. Electricity is produced by burning the fossil fuels in a thermal power station to produce steam which drives the turbines. |
| Oil | Fuel for vehicles and electricity generation. | |
| Natural gas | Electricity generation. Raw material in chemical industry. | |
| Hydro-electricity | Electricity generation. | Renewable. Produced when water is stored, usually behind a dam, and moved at speed downhill to drive a turbine. |
| Nuclear fuel:<br>Uranium | Electricity generation. | Non-renewable. Ore is mined containing a small amount of uranium which has to be extracted. |
| Timber | Fuel for cooking and domestic heat. | Renewable. |
| Alternative sources of energy | Electricity generation. | Renewable. The main alternative sources are geothermal, tidal, wave, wind and solar power. |

## 6.2 The distribution of natural resources and their exploitation and consumption

**(a) The Distribution of Natural Resources**

1. Resources are not evenly distributed throughout the world.
2. Even where a resource is widely distributed the quality of the resource varies (e.g. water supply).
3. The developed countries have more natural resources of a higher quality than those of the developing countries. For instance, most developing countries rely on their traditional energy source, fuel wood, as few possess fossil fuels or the money and technology to develop alternatives. Fuel for vehicles and electricity generation is either imported or supplied from hydro-electric schemes.

**(b) The Distribution of Exploitation**

1. Some natural resources are not exploited. Exploitation depends on the level of technology available and the demand.

2. Exploitation is the function of primary industry.
3. The same resource may be exploited more intensively in one area than another. For instance, the dangers associated with generating nuclear power and disposing of the waste products have meant that the politicians of some countries have decided not to use nuclear power while others have developed nuclear power stations on a large scale.
4. Developed countries have exploited their resources more fully than developing countries.
5. The distribution of the exploitation of a particular resource changes as demand and extractive techniques alter. For instance, competition from other energy sources has caused a reduction in the demand for coal and an increase in mechanisation. As a result there are fewer miners and inefficient mines have been closed.

### (c) The Distribution of Consumption

1. The consumption of resources is uneven.
2. The developed countries consume most of the world's extracted resources. For instance, approximately 80% of the annual world consumption of energy occurs in the developed world.
3. The movement of resources from one country to another is necessary either because a country does not possess its own or because a country does not possess enough to meet the demand. The pattern of movement depends on the location of the demand and supply of the particular resource. For instance, oil is generally moved from developing countries to the developed countries and coal is moved between developed countries.
4. In general, the mineral wealth and commercial crops produced by developing countries are moved, unprocessed, to the developed countries for use. For instance, most of the oil produced by Venezuela, China, Mexico and the countries of the Middle East is shipped for use in the developed countries.

## 6.3   The threat to natural resources

### (a) Exhaustion of Non-renewable Resources

1. Non-renewable resources at present rates of exploitation will run out. Exhaustion dates for some have already been predicted (e.g. natural gas 35 years).
2. The consumption rate of the world's energy resources has been referred to as the 'energy crisis'.

### (b) The Energy Crisis

1. The term energy crisis is being used because of the effects that a shortage of energy resources would have on the level of world development.

2. A shortage of energy resources may result because:

    (a) The consumption of energy in the world is increasing.

    (b) Most (approximately 80%) of the world's energy comes from non-renewable sources.

    (c) Most renewable energy resources are at the moment poorly developed and it is difficult to estimate whether they can produce enough energy to replace non-renewable sources when the latter run out.

    (d) HEP, the most developed renewable resource, has an estimated world potential of only 200 exajoules.

    (e) Nuclear power using plutonium and uranium in fast breeder reactors is more dangerous than the present, conventional, nuclear processes.

### (c) The Threat to Renewable Resources

1. The ability of renewable resources to be used again and again is being threatened by the activities of people.
2. Some renewable rescources are being used at a rate which does not allow them to regenerate (e.g. fuel wood).
3. The use of a resource may damage the ecosystem so that regeneration is not possible. For instance, the removal of natural vegetation for agriculture and fuel wood may cause soil erosion preventing new growth of the vegetation and the continued production of agricultural products (see Section 4.5 (b)).
4. Human activity has polluted many of the world's renewable resources, either reducing their value or making them worthless.

**Table 6.3**  Causes and effects of pollution

| Causes | Effects |
|---|---|
| Air pollution. | |
| Carbon and sulphur dioxide are released into the atmosphere when coal, oil and natural gas are burned to generate electricity and in the exhaust fumes of cars. | Sulphur dioxide combines with rain making it acidic (acid rain) so that it kills trees and fish. Together these gases create smog which blocks the sunlight, damages people's lungs and dirties buildings. |
| Smelting industries and car exhausts release toxic waste. | Damages people's health. |
| Aerosol sprays release gases. | The ozone layer that protects the earth from the harmful effects of the sun's light is attacked and its beneficial effects reduced. |
| Leaks of radiation into the air from nuclear power stations. | Radiation levels increase causing crops to die and the soil to be contaminated for an as yet unknown period of time. Animals and people suffer from radiation diseases. |

| | |
|---|---|
| Water pollution. Pesticides and fertilisers from agriculture, untreated sewage and detergents from settlements and toxic waste from industry enter rivers. | This combination reduces the oxygen in the water by increasing the growth of algae. Fish, animals and birds that depend on the river are killed and the water becomes unsafe to drink. |
| Toxic and radioactive waste, polluted rivers, oil spillage and the deliberate washing out of tankers and the litter that the tide collects as it washes beaches all combine to pollute the sea. | Fish and sea birds die and beaches are polluted as oil slicks are washed ashore. |
| Noise pollution. Noise from the operations of agriculture, industry and especially from transport. | Noise creates stress and reduces the quality of life of people who live nearby. |
| Visual pollution. Derelict and working industrial buildings, waste tips, transport links, communication masts and pylons can all be eyesores. | These reduce the scenic beauty of an area and can create a depressing environment in which to live. |

## 6.4 Conservation of natural resources

### (a) Strategies for Conserving Non-renewable Resources

1. A number of strategies are available to try to conserve the non-renewable resources of the world.
2. Waste can be reduced by recycling and by the development of better production techniques that require smaller quantities to produce the same amount of finished product.
3. Substitutes can be found, preferably renewable resources, for non-renewable resources.
4. Exploration on the earth and in space may find new deposits of non-renewable resources.

### (b) Conservation Strategies Applied to the Energy Crisis

**Table 6.4**  Conservation strategies applied to the energy crisis

| Conservation strategy | Example |
|---|---|
| 1. The elimination of waste by the producer | Improved wood-burning cooking stoves |
| 2. The elimination of waste by the consumer | Double-glazing of homes and offices |
| 3. Recycling of resources | Power stations using household refuse as a fuel |

| | |
|---|---|
| 4. Exploration of the earth and space | Exploration of Antarctica |
| 5. Conservation of renewable resources | Tree planting |
| 6. Finding alternative resources | Waste from sugar cane factories used to make alcohol as an alternative vehicle fuel in Brazil |
| 7. Developing extraction techniques | The extraction of oil from shales that contain oil |

### (c) Conservation of Renewable Resources

1. The level of pollution can be controlled but is expensive and is only usually effective when political decisions are taken to impose pollution controls.
2. More international agreements need to be made and enforced to ensure that renewable resources such as fish and timber are not used to the point where regeneration is no longer possible.
3. Some strategies to reduce the rate of use result in hardship for groups of people who are sometimes the poorer sections of the world's population.

## 6.5 Natural resources examples

**Table 6.5** Natural resources examples

| Named examples of | Factual information needed | Your named example |
|---|---|---|
| 1. A renewable resource | Name and location. Details of how it has been extracted, used and moved and by whom. | 1. |
| 2. A non-renewable resource | Name and location. Details of how it has been extracted, used and moved and by whom. | 2. |
| 3. A developed country | Name and location. Details of its natural resources and its trade in natural resources. | 3. |
| 4. A developing country | Name and location. Details of its natural resources and its trade in natural resources. | 4. |
| 5. A primary industry other than agriculture | Name and distribution of industry in a region or country. Reasons for location. Trends in production and consumption. | 5. |
| 6. A non-renewable resource that has had its exhaustion date predicted | Name and location. Details of causes and effects of exhaustion. Possible solutions. | 6. |
| 7. A renewable resource that is threatened | Name and location. Details of causes and effects of the threat. Possible solutions. | 7. |

## 6.6  Questions and answers

### (a) Structured Questions

### Example 6.1

(a) Study the graph and table below:

| Source of energy | Percentage of total energy used |
|---|---|
| Coal | 36 |
| Oil | 34 |
| Natural gas | 22 |
| Nuclear | 6 |
| Hydro-electric | 2 |

Table showing the percentages of energy supplied by different sources to a European country.

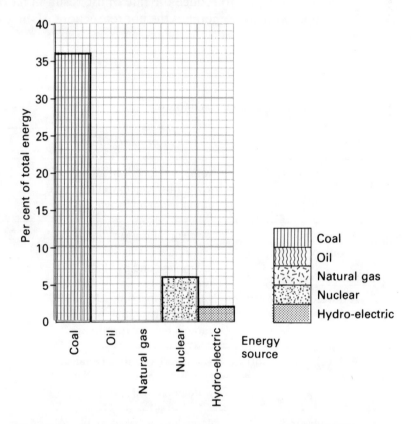

Graph showing the percentages of energy supplied by different sources to a European country

   (i) Using the information in the table complete the graph.
   (ii) State the meaning of the term non-renewable resource.
   (iii) Name two examples of non-renewable resources.

(b) A new power station is needed to produce extra energy in a country. Some people support the building of a nuclear power station and some are against.
   (i) State fully one reason against building a nuclear power station.
   (ii) State fully one reason for building a nuclear power station as opposed to another type of power station.

(c) Study the photograph below:

An urban area

(i) Label the features 1–6 taking your answers from the list below:
wooded area; high-rise flats; cul-de-sac of semi-detached housing;
river; road; block of terraced housing; large detached house

(ii) Name the resource being exploited at location X on the aerial
photograph.

(iii) State fully two arguments which a householder at Y might make
to the local council when complaining about the work at X.

(d) Until recently people were unable to exploit some of the world's
resources because the technology did not exist. In recent years advances
in technology have enabled them to exploit many of these resources.

(i) State one example of a resource which was difficult to exploit
until recently and state its location.

(ii) Explain one factor which makes the resource named in (d) (i)
above difficult to exploit.

(iii) State fully one way in which technology overcomes the factor that
you have named in (d) (ii) above.

(**NISEC** paper 1 question 1 1988)

**Solution 6.1**

(a) (i) See the figure below:

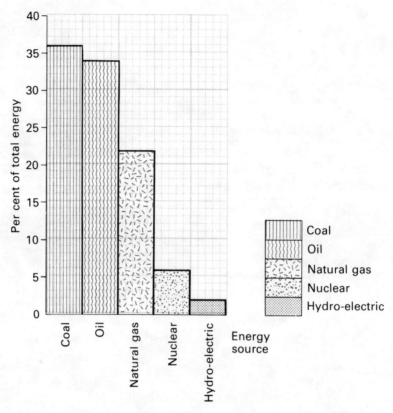

Graph showing the percentages of energy supplied by different sources to a European country

(ii) Resources are used by people. Non-renewable resources are finite resources which will eventually be exhausted.

(iii) Example 1 – coal.
Example 2 – iron ore.

(b) (i) Nuclear power stations are a risk because radioactive material may be released into the atmosphere. The increased radioactivity in the atmosphere causes contamination of water and food supplies and is thought to increase the incidence of leukaemia and other forms of cancer in humans.

(ii) A nuclear power station could be built rather than a coal-fired power station because this would reduce the amount of sulphur dioxide entering the atmosphere. The sulphur dioxide combines with rain making it more acidic. Acid rain pollutes vegetation, soil and water.

(c) (i) Feature 1 – farmland.
Feature 2 – large detached house.
Feature 3 – wooded area.
Feature 4 – block of terraced housing.
Feature 5 – cul-de-sac of semi-detached housing.
Feature 6 – road.

(ii) Sand.

(iii) **Argument 1**

The diggers that extract the sand and the lorries that leave area X opposite the house at Y, to take the sand to where it is needed, create a large amount of noise which causes stress for the householder and family. The householder Y wants the council to make the extraction company pay for noise reduction measures, e.g. double glazing, at house Y.

**Argument 2**

When a high wind is blowing from area X to house Y large amounts of dust blow towards the house making it dirty and preventing the household enjoying the use of the garden. The householder at Y wants the council to ban the use of the site at X when the above wind conditions prevail.

(d) (i) Resource – Oil.
Location – North Sea.

(ii) The depth of the North Sea, between 80 and 180 metres, made it difficult to secure the drilling platforms that were necessary to find and exploit the oil.

(iii) The development of semi-submersible drilling platforms enabled drilling operations to take place in deep water without the need for extensive supports to be attached to the sea bed.

**Example 6.2**

(a) Study the figure below:

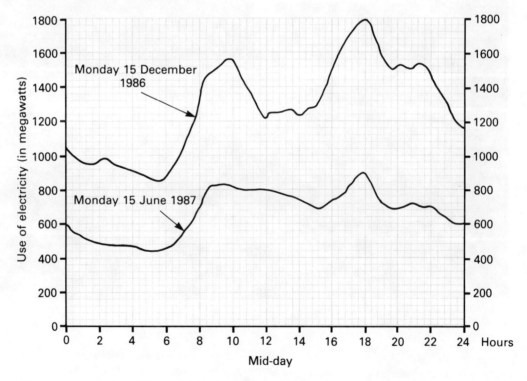

The amount of electricity used in the UK on two days

(i) What was the difference in the amounts of electricity used between 15 December and 15 June at 1800 hours (6 p.m.)?

(ii) Suggest one reason for this difference.

(iii) What difficulty, for the electricity supply industry, is shown by the pattern on the graph?

(b) Study the photograph below:

A power station scheme

What type of power station is shown?

    (c)  Study the photograph below:

Another power station scheme

Suggest two reasons why the power station was built here.
    (d)  Describe two advantages and two disadvantages of a power station like
        the one shown in the first photograph compared with a power station
        like the one in the second photograph. Use the photographs and refer
        to examples you have studied.

(**MEG** syllabus A paper 2 question 5 1988)

**Solution 6.2**

(a)  (i) 900 megawatts.

(ii) The temperature on 15 of December was lower than on 15 of June.

(iii) The difficulty shown by the pattern is that the demand for electricity varies from season to season and during the day.

(b) A hydro-electric power station.

(c) **Reason 1**

The land on which the station is built is flat.

**Reason 2**

The land may have been used for agriculture and was therefore relatively cheap to buy.

(d) **Advantage 1**

Hydro-electric power stations such as the Volta dam in Ghana use water, a renewable resource, to generate electricity. Thermal power stations, such as Didcot power station in England, use a non-renewable resource: fossil fuels.

**Advantage 2**

Hydro-electric power stations do not cause atmospheric pollution. Thermal power stations give off gases (e.g. sulphur dioxide) which pollute the atmosphere.

**Disadvantage 1**

The creation of a hydro-electric power station often causes a large amount of agricultural land to be flooded, usually far more than is needed for a thermal power station. The creation of the Volta Dam in Ghana flooded an area of approximately 8500 square kilometres

**Disadvantage 2**

Suitable sites for hydro-electric power stations are often in areas of natural beauty; station development causes visual pollution e.g. the Norsk hydro-electric power station in Norway. Thermal power stations are usually found in areas where the natural beauty of the landscape is less important, and the visual impact of the power station is often less noticeable because other developments have already taken place.

# 7 Population

## 7.1 Distribution and density

1. The **distribution** of population refers to the spread of people in an area.
2. The **density** of population is the number of people per unit area. The unit can be square kilometre, square mile, hectare or acre.

## 7.2 Factors determining the distribution and density of population

### (a) Physical Factors

1. Positive physical factors attract people to an area and allow industrial, agricultural and commercial development to take place.
2. Negative physical factors discourage people from occupying an area.

**Table 7.1** Positive and negative physical factors

| Physical factors | Positive | Negative |
|---|---|---|
| Natural route ways | Presence | Absence |
| Relief | Flat or undulating | Steep or rugged |
| Soil fertility | Fertile | Infertile |
| Natural vegetation | Lush, edible, accessible | Sparse, inedible, inaccessible |
| Climate | Wet and warm | Cold, dry |
| Mineral deposits | Presence | Absence |

3. The highest densities of population are found where positive physical factors occur as point resources (e.g. a natural harbour) or small areas (e.g. a fertile river plain).

### (b) Non-physical Factors

1. The people of an area must have the necessary human skills to further the agricultural, industrial and commercial development of the area's natural resources.
2. The relationship between population density and the development of resources is not straightforward. A low level of development does not necessarily mean a low population density, as high population densities can be sustained with a lower quality of life (see Chapter 9).
3. Some human activities (e.g. war and pollution) prevent or hinder the development of human and natural resources and can reduce the population density.

## 7.3　Overpopulation and underpopulation

### (a) Overpopulation

1. **Overpopulation** occurs when an area's population is too large to be supported by the available resources.
2. Overpopulation can result in unemployment, or even famine.
3. These problems can be lessened by a reduction in the number of people in an area, by agricultural and industrial development, and by international aid.

### (b) Underpopulation

1. **Underpopulation** occurs when an area's population is too small to make use of all the resources.
2. Different societies have different living standards and expectations. An overpopulated area in a developed country may appear to be underpopulated to a developing country.

## 7.4　Population growth

### (a) Malthus's Ideas on Population Growth

1. Malthus, in the nineteenth century, believed that population grew in a geometric way (1, 2, 4, 8, 16, 32, etc.) at a faster rate than the food supply which grew arithmetically (1, 2, 3, 4, 5, 6, etc.).
2. Total poverty would only be avoided by checks on population growth such as war, famine and disease.
3. Malthus did not account for:

   (a) the population growth rate tending to slow down before total poverty is reached and before war, famine and disease check the population
   (b) international trade and aid
   (c) the rate of improvements in farming efficiency
   (d) the development of effective birth control.

### (b) Natural Increase

1. **Natural increase** is the balance between **birth rates** and **death rates**. Both rates are measured by the number of incidences per 1000 of population in a year.
2. Natural increase is taking place rapidly (the world's population is growing) because birth rates exceed death rates.
3. Natural increase implies that more resources, or a better use of resources, are needed to avoid a drop in living standards.
4. The relationship between birth rates and death rates varies from place to place and from time to time.

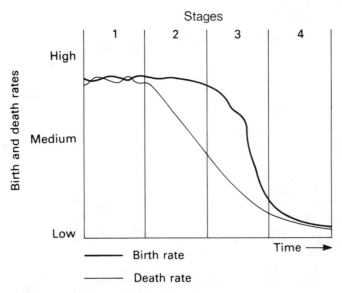

**Figure 7.1** The population cycle

**Table 7.2** Description of the population cycle

| Stage | 1 | 2 | 3 | 4 |
|---|---|---|---|---|
| Birth rate | High → | High → | High–low ↓ | Low → |
| Death rate | High → | High–medium ↓ | Medium–low ↓ | Low → |
| Population growth rate | → | ↑ rapid | ↑ rapid at start, slow at end | → |
| Stage reached by less developed countries | ● | ● | Some | |
| Stage reached by developed countries | ● | ● | ● | ● |

*Key* → steady ↓ decreasing ↑ increasing

5. Note from Fig. 7.1 that where the gap between the rise in birth rate and the fall in death rate is greatest natural increase is greatest, and that a prolonged fall in the death rate is followed by a fall in the birth rate.

**(c) Migration**

1. **Migration** is the movement of people from one area to another.
2. There are a number of different types of migration which can be grouped depending on the cause, distance, origin, destination and duration of the migration.
3. An area's population will grow if **in-migration** (people arriving in the area from other areas) is greater than **out-migration** (people leaving the area for other areas).
4. Where migrants cross a national boundary they are known as **immigrants** if entering a country and **emigrants** if leaving.

**Table 7.3** Types of migration

| | Examples 1 | 2 | 3 |
|---|:---:|:---:|:---:|
| **(a) Cause** | | | |
|    (i)  Forced | ● | | |
|    (ii) Voluntary | | ● | ● |
| **(b) Origin** | | | |
|    (i)  Rural | ● | ● | |
|    (ii) Urban | | | ● |
| **(c) Destination** | | | |
|    (i)  International – rural | ● | | |
|                 – urban | | | ● |
|    (ii) Internal     – rural | | | |
|                 – urban | | ● | |
| **(d) Duration** | | | |
|    (i)  Permanent | ● | ● | |
|    (ii) Temporary – seasonal | | | ● |
|                   – periodic | | | |

*Example 1* Refugee
Forced from a rural area to another rural area in a different country, permanent.
*Example 2* Unemployed farmer
Voluntary from a rural area to an urban area in the same country, permanent.
*Example 3* Unemployed labourer
Voluntary from an urban area to an urban area in a different country, seasonal.

## 7.5  Factors determining death rates and birth rates

### (a) Birth Rates

1. Birth rates are high if:

   (a) The population has a high percentage of young adults.
   (b) The level of education is low.
   (c) The average age for marriage is low.
   (d) A male heir to the family is important.
   (e) A religion opposes birth control.
   (f) Children form an important part of the labour force.

2. Birth rates are higher in developing countries as more of the conditions in 1. prevail.

### (b) Death Rates

1. Death rates are lowered and therefore **life expectancy** is increased by an improvement in:

(a) environmental conditions (e.g. modern sewage treatment)
(b) diet (e.g. a balanced diet)
(c) medical services (e.g. vaccination programmes).

2. Death rates are lower in developed countries as more of the conditions in 1. prevail.

## 7.6  The process and effects of migration

### (a) The Process

1. **Push** factors encourage out-migration, e.g. lack of employment.
2. **Pull** factors encourage in-migration, e.g. better accommodation.
3. The **voluntary** migrant has to balance these push and pull factors to decide if the pull of the destination is sufficient to outweigh the time, cost and social upheaval that the actual move will create.
4. The **forced** migrant considers only push factors because they are very strong and usually happen quickly.
5. Migration tends to be selective, most migrants being young, male adults of a limited number of races.

### (b) The Effects

Migrants have an effect on the area that they leave (e.g. rural depopulation) and on the area that they go to (e.g. the creation of multi-racial and multi-ethnic societies).

## 7.7  Population characteristics

### (a) Ways of Grouping

Populations are grouped according to:

1. population structure (age and sex)
2. religion
3. language
4. nationality
5. occupational structure (type of job)
6. race

### (b) Population Structure

1. **Population structure** is the percentage of males and females in different age groupings. It is usually shown by a **population pyramid**.
2. A population pyramid is the result of a population's birth and death rates and the amount of in and out migration.
3. The two major types of population pyramids are discussed in Section 7.9 (a) Question 4.

## 7.8 Population examples

**Table 7.4** Population examples

| Named examples of | Factual information needed | Your named example |
|---|---|---|
| 1. An area of low population density | | 1. |
| 2. An area of high population density: developed country | Density values, reasons (physical and non-physical) | 2. |
| 3. An area of high population density: less developed country | | 3. |
| 4. An area where the problems of overpopulation have been lessened by better use of resources | Density values, description of agricultural, industrial change causing better use of resources | 4. |
| 5. A country which has a progressive population pyramid | Description of a pyramid, reasons for characteristics, likely effect on future structure | 5. |
| 6. A country which has a regressive population pyramid | | 6. |
| 7. Birth rates and death rates of a less developed country | Stage on population cycle, facts about trends and reasons for trends, rate of population growth | 7. |
| 8. Birth rates and death rates of a developed country | | 8. |
| 9. Example of a forced migration | Origin, destinations, amount of migration and push factors | 9. |
| 10. Example of a voluntary migration | Origin, destinations, amount of migration, push and pull factors | 10. |
| 11. An area of out-migrations | Type and number of people leaving, effects on population structure and development | 11. |
| 12. An area of in-migrations | Type and number of people leaving, effects on population structure and development | 12. |

# 7.9 Questions and answers

## (a) Multiple-choice and Completion Questions

**1** During the last twenty years many young people have moved from the rural areas of 'developing' countries to the large cities mainly because:

    **A** Good housing is available for factory workers.
    **B** Tribal custom encourages them to move.
    **C** Governments encourage them to move.
    **D** Factories are short of workers.
    **E** They think that well-paid jobs are available.

                                       (**LEAG** syllabus A (specimen) question 4)

**2** Which of the following definitions best describes the term underpopulation?

    **A** An area's population is too small.
    **B** An area's population uses the available resources fully.
    **C** An area's population is too small to use the available resources fully.
    **D** An area's population has enough resources to survive.
    **E** An area's population is too large.

**3** Which one of the following is not a physical factor?

    **A** climate
    **B** relief
    **C** soil
    **D** road
    **E** mineral deposit

**4** Look at the figure below:

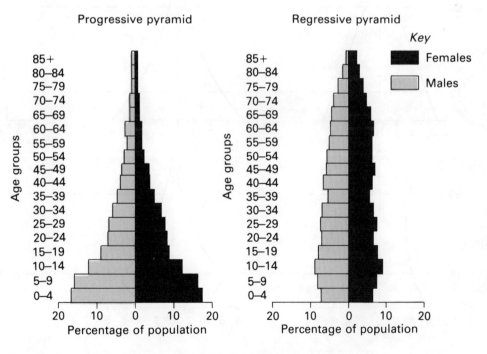

Progressive and regressive population pyramids

93

Complete the table below by putting the correct word or phrase in the correct column:

Description of progressive and regressive population pyramids

| Type of pyramid | | Progressive | Regressive |
|---|---|---|---|
| Type of country | Developing or developed? | *Developing* | *Developed* |
| Size of pyramid top | Narrow or wide? | *Nar* | *W* |
| Probable death rate | High or low? | *H* | *L* |
| Probable infant death rate | High or low? | *H* | *L* |
| Probable life expectancy | Short or long? | *S* | *L* |
| Size of pyramid base | Wide or narow, increasing or decreasing? | *W d* | *N i* |
| Probable birth rate | High or low, increasing or decreasing? | *H d* | *L i* |

**5** Look at the figure below:

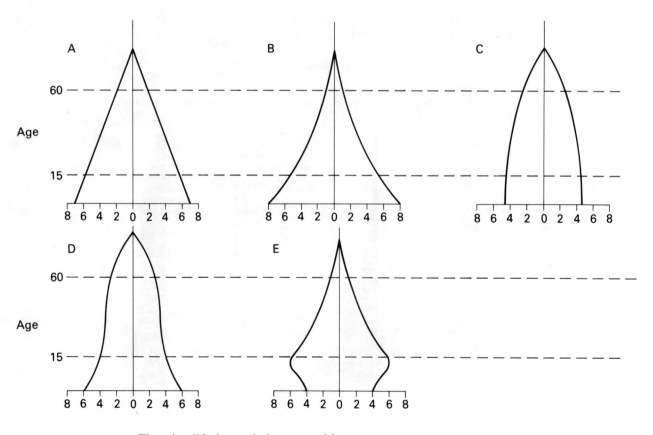

Five simplified population pyramids

Complete the table below by putting the correct population pyramid letter (**A–E**) beside the correct description:

Description of five population pyramids

| Descriptions | Pyramid letter |
|---|---|
| 1. A country with low birth rates and death rates | A ✗C |
| 2. A country which has experienced a marked and rapid decline in its birth rate | E ✓ |
| 3. A country with high birth and death rates | B ✓ |
| 4. A country with low birth rate and death rates which now has an increasing birth rate | D ✓ |
| 5. A country with high birth rates and falling death rates | C ✗ A |

### (b) Structured Questions

### Example 7.1

(a) Look at the figure below:

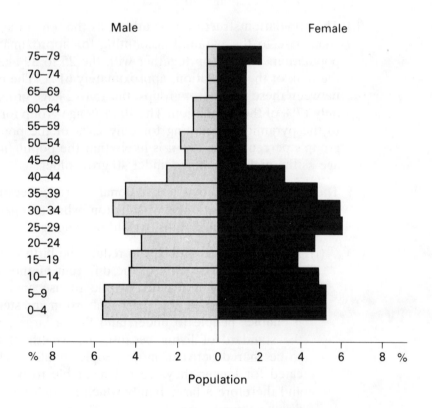

The age and sex structure of Washington, a New Town in north-east England

     (i) What percentage of males are aged between 45 and 49 years old?
    (ii) What percentage of the population are aged between 70 and 74?
   (iii) Which age group has the largest percentage of the population?
   (iv) What is the difference between the percentage of the population aged between 20 to 24 and 10 to 14?

(b) Describe the age structure of Washington.

(c) The birth rate for Washington is above the national average. Explain this statement by using evidence from the pyramid.

(d) Explain how the birth rate can be reduced in a less developed country by

    (i) improved education

    (ii) increased mechanisation of agriculture.

**Solution 7.1**

(a)    (i) 1.6% of the population are aged between 45 and 49 years old.

    (ii) 1.8% of the population are aged between 70 and 74.

    (iii) The 30 to 34 age group contains the largest percentage of the population.

    (iv) The percentage difference between the two age groups is found by subtracting the largest age group (10 to 14) from the smallest age group (20 to 24).

        10–14 age group = 9.7% of the population
        20–24 age group = 8.3% of the population

        The percentage difference = 9.7 − 8.3 = 1.4%

(b) The population structure is youthful, as the 0 to 14 age group forms a wide base to the pyramid accounting for approximately 31% of the population. This group together with the 25 to 39 age group contains the bulk of the population, approximately 61%. The pyramid narrows between these two major groups, the 15 to 24 age group accounting for only 17% of the population. The 40 to 79 age group forms a narrow top to the pyramid, accounting for only 23% of the population. As this group's percentage is low it is likely that the population structure will age as the high percentage under 40 grow older.

(c) The birth rate is above the national average because a large percentage of the population of Washington, when compared to the rest of the country, are female adults of child-bearing age.

(d)    (i) Improved education helps to reduce the birth rate because, firstly, it makes people aware of the different methods of family planning; secondly it teaches people to use contraceptive devices and understand the true risks of abortion and sterilisation; thirdly it enables people to understand that a large population lowers the standard of living because the wealth of the country has to be shared between more people; finally if children are educated for longer they are not available to work for the family and therefore a large family which needs supporting becomes a disadvantage.

    (ii) In many less developed countries children form an important part of the agricultural labour force and therefore large families are an advantage. An increase in mechanisation of agriculture lessens the need for child labour by reducing the time it takes to do a farming job. Adults now have the time to do the jobs that children used to do. A large family becomes a disadvantage because it needs feeding and clothing but is no longer used as the workforce.

**Example 7.2**

(a) Look at the figure below:

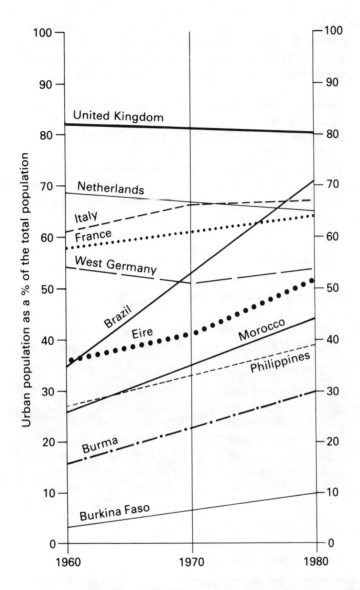

The change in urban population of selected countries 1960–1980

(i) How many countries have increased their urban population from 1960 to 1980?

(ii) Name the countries that had a decrease in their urban population.

(iii) In which country has the percentage urban population increased the most from 1960 to 1980 and by how much?

(b) Read the passage below:

---

*Counter urbanisation*

In the 1960s fewer people migrated to the cities of the USA than in previous decades. In fact for the first time there was a greater proportion of people leaving many major American cities than moving into them. **Counter urbanisation** had begun. In several European countries the same trend started in the 1970s.

The steady movement of people to large towns and cities of Western Europe which had been a major demographic feature of the 19th and early 20th centuries is slowing down or in some cases reversing in the later part of the 20th century.

One Western European country where the percentage of the population living in urban areas has decreased between 1960 and 1980 is the Netherlands.

---

Urban population change, 1970–1980, in selected cities of the Netherlands

**Cities with populations over 150 000**

| City | Population 1970 | Population 1980 | % Increase or decrease |
|------|-----------------|-----------------|------------------------|
| Amsterdam | 831 500 | 712 300 | −14.3 |
| Rotterdam | 686 600 | 576 300 | −16.1 |
| The Hague | 550 600 | 456 700 | −17.1 |
| Utrecht | 279 000 | 236 200 | −15.3 |
| Eindhoven | 188 600 | 195 700 | + 3.8 |
| Haarlem | 172 000 | 157 600 | − 8.4 |
| Groningen | 168 800 | 163 000 | − 3.4 |
| Tilburg | 152 600 | 153 100 | + 0.3 |

**Cities with populations under 150 000**

| City | Population 1970 | Population 1980 | % Increase or decrease |
|------|-----------------|-----------------|------------------------|
| Nijmegen | 148 800 | 147 300 | − 1.0 |
| Enschede | 139 200 | 144 300 | + 3.7 |
| Apeldoarn | 123 600 | 140 800 | +13.9 |
| Zaanstad | 116 100 | 129 700 | +11.7 |
| Arnhem | 132 500 | 128 700 | − 2.9 |
| Breda | 121 200 | 117 100 | − 3.4 |
| Maastricht | 93 900 | 110 200 | +17.4 |
| Dordrecht | 88 700 | 108 000 | +21.8 |
| Leiden | 101 200 | 103 200 | + 2.0 |

(i) Using the information in the passage and tables above, describe the pattern of change in the urban population of the Netherlands.

(ii) Using the headings given below suggest why many large cities in Europe and North America are losing population:

A the crime rate
B pollution
C increased car ownership
D improved transport networks
E changing standards of living/increasing affluence.

(c) Look at the figure below:

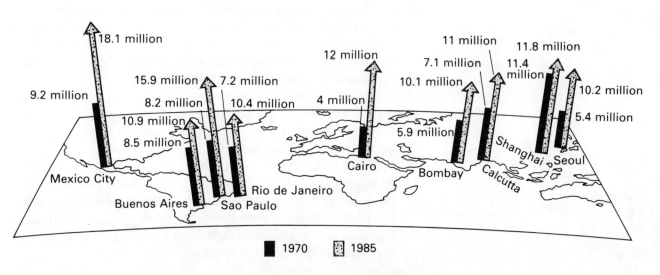

1970    1985

The nine fastest expanding cities in the world and the rate at which populations have increased from 1970 to 1985

Some of the Third World cities have doubled their populations since 1970. What problems does this cause for the governments in the countries concerned?

(MEG syllabus C paper 2 question 5 1988)

**Solution 7.2**

(a)    (i) Eight countries have increased their urban population from 1960 to 1980.
    (ii) United Kingdom, Netherlands and West Germany.
  (iii) Brazil by 36%.

(b)    (i) The passage states that the percentage of the population living in urban areas in the Netherlands has decreased between 1960 and 1980. The tables show how the urban population change of cities varies depending on the size of the city. Apart from the exceptions of Eindhoven and Tilburg, which have had a percentage increase of 3.8 and 0.3 respectively, the other large cities with populations of over 150 000 have had a percentage decrease. The percentage decrease varies from 3.4 in the case of Groningen to 17.1 in the case of The Hague.

In cities of less than 150 000 this pattern is reversed. Six of the ten cities have had a percentage increase ranging from 3.7 at Enschede to 21.8 at Dordrecht.

(ii) **A** The crime rate in large cities may be higher than in smaller settlements and rural areas. The greater risk of attack and/or damage to property has encouraged people to leave large cities.

**B** The greater concentration of residential and industrial buildings and vehicles may cause more noise, air and visual pollution in larger settlements so people prefer to live in smaller settlements where pollution is less.

**C** An increase in car ownership increases the mobility of the population by making them less dependent on public transport. People are able to leave large cities and still travel to work in them, and are able to use cars to obtain services in rural areas where public transport is limited.

**D** Improved transport networks may reduce the journey time for travel. This encourages people to leave large cities because they can live away from the city but can still travel to the city for work and entertainment.

**E** One way that the standard of living may be changing is a result of increased leisure time. This may encourage people to look for a better leisure environment than large cities can offer. Increasing affluence may mean that more people can afford to buy a car and spend more money on travelling to work and are therefore able to leave a large city.

(c) The rapid growth of population in some cities has meant that a high percentage of the population are unemployed or have poorly paid jobs, often in the informal sector (see Section 13.2), and many people are housed in substandard accommodation (sometimes called shanty towns) which have only limited services. In order to remedy these problems the government needs to invest money into housing, services and the creation of jobs. Unfortunately the financial resources of the concerned governments are inadequate because of the scale of the problems.

(c) **Answers to Multiple-choice and Completion Questions**

**1 E**
**2 C**
**3 D**

**4** See the table below:

Description of progressive and regressive population pyramids

| Type of pyramid | Progressive | Regressive |
| --- | --- | --- |
| Type of country | Developing | Developed |
| Size of pyramid top | Narrow | Wide |
| Probable death rate | High | Low |
| Probable infant death rate | High | Low |
| Probable life expectancy | Short | Long |
| Size of pyramid base | Wide and increasing | Narrow and decreasing |
| Probable birth rate | High and increasing | Low and decreasing |

**5** See the table below:

Description of five population pyramids

| Descriptions | Pyramid letter |
| --- | --- |
| 1. A country with low birth rates and death rates | C |
| 2. A country which has experienced a marked and rapid decline in its birth rate | E |
| 3. A country with high birth and death rates | B |
| 4. A country with low birth rate and death rates which now has an increasing birth rate | D |
| 5. A country with high birth rates and falling death rates | A |

# 8 Settlement

## 8.1 Growth and decline of settlements

### (a) The Function of Settlements

1. Settlements exist to perform certain **functions** or jobs that are carried out more efficiently if people and buildings are grouped together in a central place. The basic functions of settlements are to provide the services and work that people need.
2. Sometimes a dominant function can be recognised (e.g. a holiday resort).
3. The particular function of a settlement can sometimes be deduced from looking at its **form** or shape, its **site** (the area of land on which the settlement is built) and its **situation** (its position in relation to surrounding physical and human features).

### (b) Settlement Growth

1. The initial choice of site reflects the needs of the occupants of the settlement (e.g. the need for defence can lead to a hilltop site).
2. Settlements have grown from this initial site by the addition of buildings on the edge of the existing development. This sometimes creates roughly circular zones, each zone representing a different phase of building.
3. The growth of a settlement depends on how successful it is at attracting people and functions. This depends to some extent on the suitability of its initial site and its situation.
4. The site and situation also affect the settlement's ability to adapt to the changing functions that it has to perform. If it does not adapt, stagnation or decline may result.

### (c) Variations in the Rate of Urban Growth

1. The quickest urban growth has been and is associated with the process of **urbanisation** which results in a greater percentage of a country's population living in urban areas.
2. In the developed world the period of fast urban growth and urbanisation in the 19th century resulted from the development of 'modern industry' and trade which attracted people from rural areas to work in the new factories which grew up in certain settlements.
3. In the developing world urban growth and urbanisation are proceeding rapidly. This is partly as a result of rural to urban migration caused by the low living standards in the rural areas and the promise of something better in the urban areas, but also as a result of the rate of natural increase in the urban areas themselves.

4. Urban growth in the developing world tends to be concentrated in a small number of cities, so that a majority of the world's cities over 3 million people are now found in the developing countries.

## 8.2   The distribution of settlement

### (a)  Distribution on the Land Surface

1. A **nucleated** pattern of settlement exists if the individual dwellings are grouped together to form a hamlet or village.
2. A **dispersed** pattern of settlement exists if the individual buildings are scattered throughout an area.
3. Some factors encourage dispersion (e.g. large farm size), and some nucleation (e.g. where land is owned by the community rather than individuals).

### (b)  Distribution in a Hierarchy

1. A **hierarchy** of settlement divides settlements into a number of categories depending on how important they are (e.g. city, town, village, hamlet).
2. Importance is usually measured by the population but a variety of indicators can be used (see Fig. 8.1).

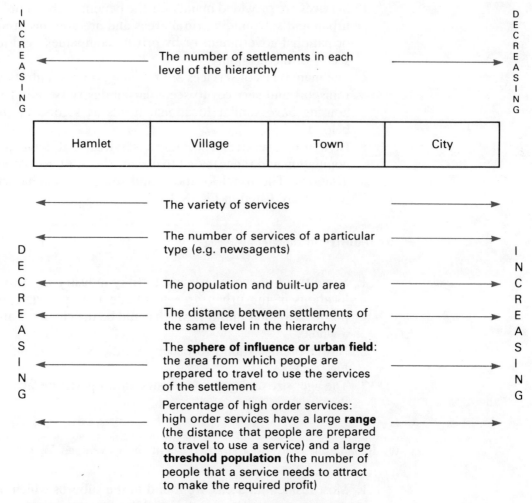

Figure 8.1   The characteristics of a hierarchy of settlement

# 8.3 Urban structure in the developed world

### (a) Functional Zones

The land use in urban areas is not haphazard, but organised into functional zones, where one type of land use is dominant.

### (b) Causes of the Functional Zones and their Location

1. Some functional zones attract and others repel each other, thus affecting the location of functional zones.
2. Land values vary in the urban area as a result of variations in accessibility. As the accessibility of land increases so does its value.
3. Some land uses need a high level of accessibility to operate efficiently so are prepared to pay to use the expensive, accessible land. Functional zones are created when similar land uses, that have the same need and ability to pay for the accessible land, group together.
4. Generally services occupy the land of highest value, followed by industry and then residential land uses.

### (c) Services in the Urban Area

1. Services are provided mainly for the benefit of the people who live in the urban and surrounding rural areas and are administered either by local or national government or by private companies, and form the tertiary sector of the economy.
2. The main types of services are retailing, offices, entertainment, welfare, transport and services to secondary industry (some of these e.g. warehousing have similar locational needs as secondary industry; see (d) below).
3. **High order services** (i.e. those services that have a high threshold population and range) need to occupy the most accessible and expensive locations. The usual locations and some of the characteristic types of services are listed in Fig. 8.2.

### (d) Industry in the Urban Area

1. Some types of secondary and tertiary industry need to be in accessible locations in the urban area to obtain raw materials and to distribute products to their market, which could be the city itself and the country as a whole.
2. Newer premises tend to occupy locations of medium accessibility (see Fig. 8.2).
3. The age, size and type of industry varies partly because of its location in the city.

### (e) Residential Zones in Urban Areas in the Developed World

1. Most residential areas are found in the suburbs which occupy the areas of lowest accessibility (see Fig. 8.2).

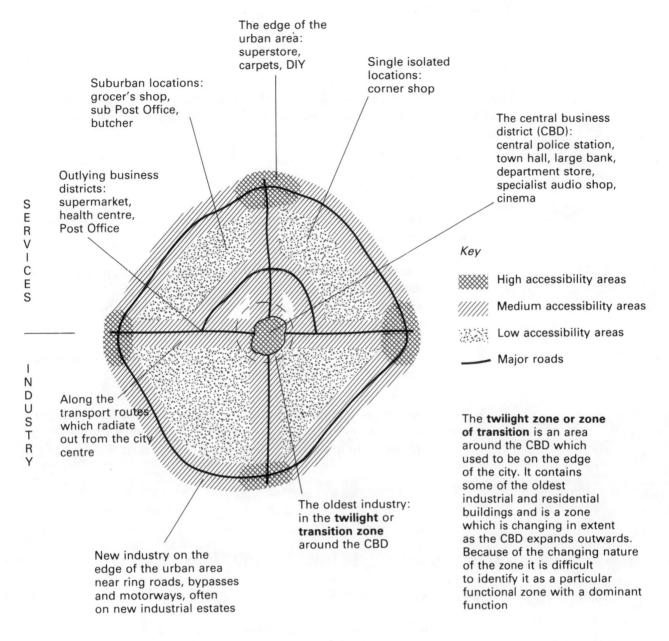

The edge of the urban area: superstore, carpets, DIY

Single isolated locations: corner shop

Suburban locations: grocer's shop, sub Post Office, butcher

The central business district (CBD): central police station, town hall, large bank, department store, specialist audio shop, cinema

Outlying business districts: supermarket, health centre, Post Office

S E R V I C E S

I N D U S T R Y

Key

High accessibility areas

Medium accessibility areas

Low accessibility areas

Major roads

Along the transport routes which radiate out from the city centre

The **twilight zone or zone of transition** is an area around the CBD which used to be on the edge of the city. It contains some of the oldest industrial and residential buildings and is a zone which is changing in extent as the CBD expands outwards. Because of the changing nature of the zone it is difficult to identify it as a particular functional zone with a dominant function

New industry on the edge of the urban area near ring roads, bypasses and motorways, often on new industrial estates

The oldest industry: in the **twilight** or **transition zone** around the CBD

**Figure 8.2** Variations in accessibility and the preferred locations of services and industry in urban areas

2. In many societies, housing is allocated depending on wealth. Where this happens the wealthiest people have the first choice of the available existing housing and the locations for new building. Historically the most favoured location has been the edge of the city where the journey to work in the city centre is compensated for by a better environment and access to the countryside.

3. As the city has expanded outwards the wealthiest people have tended to move outwards to remain on the edge of the city, leaving their original houses to be occupied by people of lower wealth.

4. The continued building of new houses on the edge has created the pattern of decreasing age of building with distance from the city centre.

5. In some societies housing owned by the state has distorted this pattern. Low-income groups occupy areas which would be favoured by high-income groups.

## 8.4   Urban structure in developing countries

### (a) Functional Zones

The main types of functional zones that are found in the urban areas in developed countries are also found in the urban areas of the developing countries.

### (b) Accessibility and Land Values

1. Accessibility and land values tend to decrease with distance from the centre because:

   (a) Public transport is poorly developed so the urban centre is difficult to reach from the edge.
   (b) The transport networks are not as developed (e.g. fewer ring roads and underground railways).

2. This causes the location of functional zones to be different from their location in urban areas in the developed world.

3. The movement of people within the residential zones of the urban areas tends to be from the edge towards the centre, although the wealthiest sometimes move to low-density, high-quality areas near the edge of the city.

## 8.5   Problems of urban areas and possible solutions

### (b) Inequalities in Service Provision

1. The uneven distribution of services causes inequality as some sections of the community find it harder to use the services because of either distance or the cost of travel.
2. The poorer sections of the community are most vulnerable because:

   (a) They have less money to spend on travel.
   (b) They are less likely to own a car and are therefore dependent on public transport.
   (c) Housing for low-income groups is sometimes on the edge of the urban area furthest away from the high-order services at the centre, e.g. the shanty towns of developing cities.

### (b) Inequalities in Housing Provision

1. Inequalities in housing provision exist because housing in many societies is allocated depending on wealth.
2. The poorest sections of the community are either homeless or forced to live in crowded substandard housing.

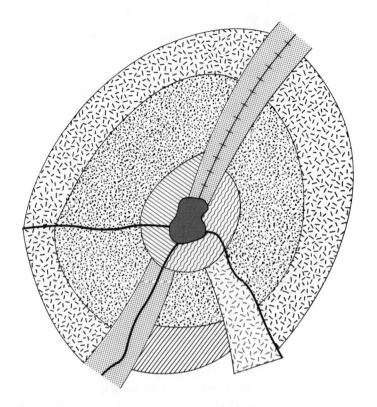

 CBD: contains modern high-rise buildings; the main shops and offices of the city. Sometimes part of the CBD is made up of an old traditional sector and/or an old colonial sector

 A zone of modern expensive high-rise apartments close to the CBD

 Modern industrial zones are generally located on the major transport routes which radiate out from the centre. They cover a smaller percentage of the urban area than in developed countries because the level of economic development tends not to promote as much traditional industry based in fixed premises

 A zone of high-quality suburban housing close to a major transport route for access to the CBD

 A zone of improved squatter settlements which are more permanent is found in a zone immediately inside the squatter settlements on the edge of the urban area

 A zone of low-cost sites and services schemes built by the government to try to begin to solve the problem of squatter settlements

 Large areas of squatter settlements that have no legal right to occupy the land (**favelas, shanty towns etc.**) grow up on any unused land, usually on the edge of the urban area because of poor access to the centre

 A zone of poor-quality housing that consists of subdivided properties that used to be high-quality housing

**Figure 8.3**   A model of the location of functional zones in urban areas in developing countries

3. The process of rapid urbanisation currently taking place in many developing countries has increased inequality because many of the migrants have to live in shanty towns. The provision of basic sites and services by governments in developing countries is an attempt to solve the problem of shanty towns.

### (c) Urban Sprawl

1. Unchecked development of low building-density suburbs causes problems:

   (a) wasteful use of agricultural land on the edge of the urban area
   (b) increased journey time in and out of the city.

2. Planning solutions include:

   (a) green belts or green corridors where new building is restricted
   (b) the creation of new towns or expanding towns where growth is diverted from the large urban areas.

3. While the planning solutions have restricted urban sprawl they have only partially reduced journey to work times. This is because the new and expanded towns have not always attracted enough employment to remove the need for commuting.

### (d) Inner City Decay

1. The Central Business District and transition zone contain some of the oldest housing and industrial buildings.
2. Old industrial properties are often derelict or not in the best position to operate efficiently.
3. The housing is often subdivided into small units which are overcrowded. Sometimes the occupants are predominantly from a minority ethnic group and so racial tension can develop.
4. **Redevelopment** occurs when old property is demolished and rebuilt and **refurbishment** when old properties are renovated; both solutions are commonly tried.
5. Both solutions can cause injustices if the interests of the residents are not taken into account.

### (e) Traffic in Urban Areas

See Section 10.5(b).

### (f) Employment

1. Levels of unemployment and employment on low wages are high amongst those who live in the poorest accommodation in the city.
2. The poor accommodation combined with the lack of employment prospects can lead to human despair.

# 8.6 Problems of rural settlement

### (a) Rural Depopulation

1. The percentage of people living in rural areas has declined partly as a result of rural to urban migration. (See section 7.4(c).)
2. This depopulation has caused problems for rural areas:

   (a) Services have been reduced because there are no longer enough people to support them.
   (b) The population of rural areas is ageing as it tends to be the young that move. In the developing countries this means a reduction in the labour force for agriculture.

### (b) Counter Urbanisation

1. In developed countries some people are leaving the urban areas to live in rural areas. This process is known as **counter urbanisation**.
2. The increased demand for property has meant a rise in house prices which the local people cannot afford.
3. Sometimes the migrants work and spend their money in the urban area, causing a reduction in the quality of rural services.

# 8.7 Settlement examples

**Table 8.1** Settlement examples

| Named examples of | Factual information needed | Your named example |
|---|---|---|
| 1. A rural settlement | Name and location, description of its site, situation and form (sketch map), list of functions | 1. |
| 2. A growth settlement | Name and location, description of structure, and reasons for growth | 2. |
| 3. A developed country that has experienced urbanisation | Name and location, details of the time and rate of the process, causes and effects of the process | 3. |
| 4. A developing country that is experiencing urbanisation | Name and location, details of the time and rate of the process, causes and effects of the process | 4. |
| 5. Area of dispersed settlement | Name and location, description of settlement pattern and reasons for pattern | 5. |
| 6. Area of nucleated settlement | Name and location, description of settlement pattern and reasons for pattern | 6. |

| | | |
|---|---|---|
| 7. Settlements at different levels in a hierarchy | Name and location of city, town, village, hamlet; description of characteristics of each | 7.(a)<br>7.(b)<br>7.(c)<br>7.(d) |
| 8. City in a developed country | Name and location; description of structure, the characteristics of functional zones, the variations in accessibility, recent changes; the problems (e.g. transport, inequalities, sprawl, inner city decay) and any improvement schemes (e.g. redevelopment and/or refurbishment, green belts or wedges) | 8. |
| 9. City in a developing country | Name and location; description of structure, the characteristics of functional zones, the variations in accessibility, recent changes; the problems (e.g. transport, inequalities, squatter settlements, employment) and any improvement schemes (e.g. sites and services) | 9. |
| 10. A new town | Name and location; details of the structure, history of development and advantages of location | 10. |
| 11. Areas of rural settlement | Name and location; description of services and functions of the settlement and related problems | 11. |

## 8.8  Questions and answers

### (a) Multiple-choice and Completion Questions

**1** For this question one or more of the responses given are correct. Decide which of the responses is (are) correct. Then choose:

**A** if 1, 2 and 3 are all correct
**B** if 1 and 2 only are correct
**C** if 2 and 3 only are correct
**D** if 1 only is correct
**E** if 3 only is correct.

Which of the following is/are a feature of the central business district of a modern city?

1. The land is used intensively
2. The percentage of residential buildings is low.
3. The amount of open space is limited.

**2** Which statement best describes the site of village Y shown below?

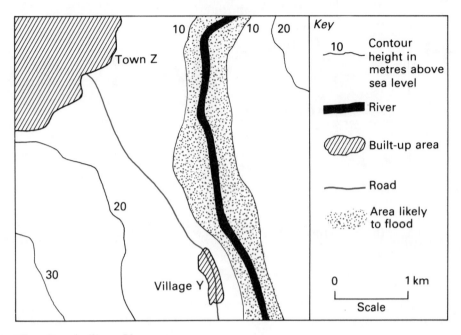

The site of village Y

    **A** It is connected to town Z by a road.
    **B** It is a linear shape.
    **C** It is approximately 3 kilometres from town Z.
    **D** It is above the area that is likely to flood.
    **E** It is on steep land.

**3** Which statement is true of a small settlement?

    **A** Its services have a long range.
    **B** Its threshold population is large.
    **C** Its sphere of influence is small.
    **D** People travel a long way to use its services.
    **E** Most of its services are middle-order.

**4** Which is the name given to zone 1 in the figure below?

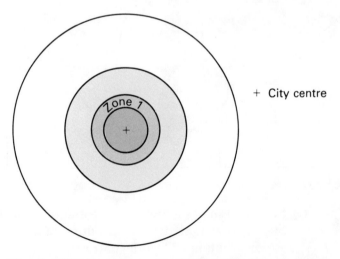

The simplified structure of a city in a developed country

A The outer suburbs.
B The central business district.
C The transition zone.
D The inner suburbs.
E The rural urban fringe.

5 Which statement is never true of the process of redevelopment?

A Homes are knocked down.
B Tower blocks are built.
C The original community is split up.
D Homes are renovated.
E Slums are cleared.

## (b) Structured Questions

### Example 8.1

(a) Look at the map below:

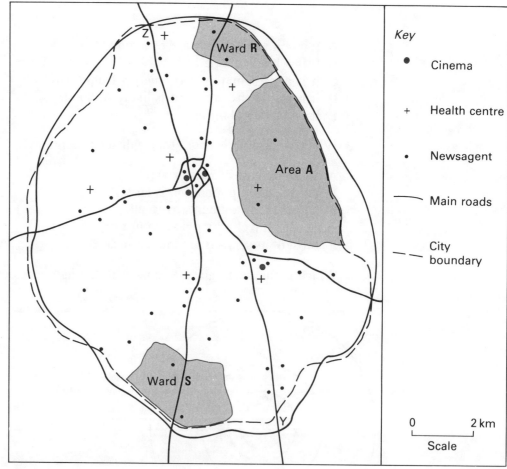

A British city

    (i) State two things about the distribution of health centres.
   (ii) State two ways that the distribution of cinemas is different from the distribution of health centres.
  (iii) Explain the differences that you have described.

(iv) Why is the number of cinemas less than the number of newsagents?

(v) Suggest a reason why there are only a few newsagents in the shaded area A.

(vi) Explain why the people living in ward R have better access to services in the city centre than those living in ward S.

(b) Look at the table below:

Selected statistics for wards R and S

|  | Ward S | Ward R |
|---|---|---|
| Persons per hectare | 68 | 18 |
| % of men aged between 16 and 64 out of employment | 16 | 9 |
| % of households which are owner occupied | 20 | 63 |
| % of households with a car | 53 | 62 |

(i) How are the figures for car ownership likely to affect access to services in the city centre for people living in wards R and S?

(ii) 'The people in ward R have more money than the people in ward S.' Use the figures in rows 1, 2 and 3 to support this statement.

(iii) Explain why people with more money have better access to services.

(c) Look at the photograph below:

Part of the shopping facilities at point Y on the map of a British city

(i) Complete the table below to show how you would expect the facilities for shoppers at the city centre to be different by crossing out the wrong words.

The characteristics of shopping centres at point Y and in the city centre

| Characteristic | Point Y | City centre |
|---|---|---|
| The number of shops | 3 | More/less |
| The variety of goods on sale | DIY, furniture, food, clothes | More/less |
| The sphere of influence of the centres | Medium | Large/medium/small |
| The cost of parking | Free | Free/charges |
| The ease of parking | Easy | Easy/difficult |
| The price of land per square metre | Medium | High/medium/low |

(ii) What are the advantages of this type of location for superstore companies?

(d) A development similar to that at location Y has been proposed at location Z. Why might a local resident object to the scheme?

## Solution 8.1

(a) (i) The health centres are distributed throughout the city. Five of the seven health centres are between 2 and 4 kilometres from the city centre.

(ii) Three of the four cinemas are grouped together. Three of the four cinemas are in the city centre.

(iii) Cinemas are private high-order services that need to be accessible to a large number of people from within and outside the city boundary; they are grouped together in the place of highest accessibility, the city centre. Health centres are public middle-order services that need to be easily accessible to all the people of the city; their even distribution mid-way between the city centre and the city boundary means that no individual living in the city has far to travel.

(iv) Newsagents are low-order services and need only a low threshold population to make a reasonable profit; cinemas are high-order services that need a high threshold population.

(v) The small number of newsagents in area A may be because the population density of area A is low.

(vi) Ward R has better access to the services of the city centre because it is nearer to the centre than ward S (4 kilometres compared with 6 kilometres), so the journey time and cost are likely to be less.

(b) (i) 62% of people living in ward R have the choice of using a car, compared with 53% in ward S; they are therefore not as dependent on public transport for getting to the centre; they can leave and return when they want.

(ii) The figures indicate that the people living in ward R have more money because fewer people are unemployed (9% in ward R compared with 16% in ward S) and more people own their own house (63% in ward R compared with 20% in ward S). The lower population density in ward S (18 people per hectare compared with 68 people per hectare in ward S) suggests that the houses in ward S are larger and have fewer people in them.

(iii) People with more money have better access to services because the cost of travelling to the services is less important. This means that they can afford to travel further, more often and have a wider selection of service centres to choose from. When they arrive at a service centre they have access to a wider choice of purchases because they can afford to pay for them.

(c)   (i) See the table below:

The characteristics of shopping centres at point Y and in the city

| Characteristic | Point Y | City centre |
|---|---|---|
| The number of shops | 3 | More/~~less~~ |
| The variety of goods on sale | DIY, furniture, food, clothes | More/~~less~~ |
| The sphere of influence of the centres | Medium | Large/~~medium/small~~ |
| The cost of parking | Free | ~~free~~/charges |
| The ease of parking | Easy | ~~easy~~/difficult |
| The price of land per square metre | Medium | High/~~medium/low~~ |

(ii) Superstores are large-scale operations that have a large amount of money invested in them. They need a large area of land and have a large threshold population so they need to be accessible. The advantage of a location close to a ring road is that it allows a large number of people to have easy access. Customers from the far side of the city can reach the site without travelling through the congested city centre. Customers from outside the city boundary do not need to enter the city, again reducing journey time and congestion.

Another advantage of a location on the edge of the city is that the land has often not been developed and a large site can be purchased and developed for a relatively low price.

(d) A local resident may object to the scheme, firstly because the development would increase the number of cars and lorries in the area increasing the danger to pedestrians, the congestion and noise and air pollution. Secondly the building itself may be an eyesore, spoiling the views from the resident's house. Thirdly the development may compete with local stores and the different type of service that these offer (e.g. home delivery) may disappear if they are forced to close. Fourthly the value of the resident's house may decrease as a result of the reduction in the quality of the environment. Finally, the development may attract other new stores to the area which would add to the problems mentioned already.

**Example 8.2**

(a) Look at the 1:50 000 map extract at the back of the book and the figure below:

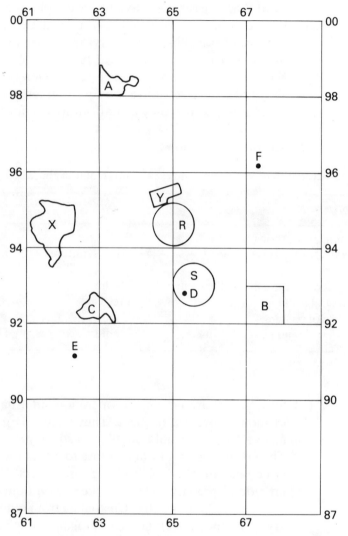

Grid of the Swansea area

(i) Name the main type of land use in the areas labelled A to C.
(ii) What land use is found at the points labelled D to F on the map?
(iii) Mark and label clearly the position of the marina (6592) and the hospital (6593) on the figure above.
(iv) Give a 6-figure grid reference for the county hall, which is located close to the marina.
(v) Add the A483 (T) from grid reference 621993 to 649947 on to the figure above.

(b) (i) Give map evidence to describe the number and variety of educational buildings.
(ii) List four other functions of the city of Swansea and give one piece of map evidence that indicates each of them.

(c) Look at areas X and Y on the figure above.
   (i) State three ways that the layout of the streets and houses in area X is different from that in area Y.
   (ii) Give and explain two pieces of map evidence that suggest that the houses in area X are newer than the houses in area Y.

(d) Look at the photographs below:

Two photographs showing the land use at grid reference 654924 at different times

1979

1986

   (i) How has the land use changed in the area?
   (ii) Name the process that has taken place.
   (iii) Explain two reasons why this process occurs in the transition zone of a city.

(e) Two areas are ringed on the grid of the Swansea area and labelled R and S. Choose the area that you think is the central business district (CBD) of Swansea. Explain your choice by using evidence from the map.

## Solution 8.2

   (a)  (i) Land use at A – mixed woodland
           Land use at B – docks
           Land use at C – park or ornamental gardens
        (ii) Land use at D – bus or coach station
           Land use at E – golf course or links
           Land use at F – multiple or single railway line with embankment

117

(iii) See the figure below:

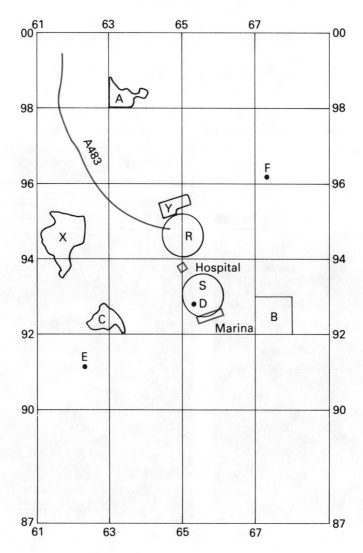

Grid of the Swansea area

 

(iv) 652923
(v) See the figure above.

(b)   (i) The map shows that there is both a large number and variety of educational establishments in the city. There are six schools (e.g. 613930), two colleges (635936 and 628934), a university (630920) and a museum (661927).

  (ii) **Function 1**

Industrial – industrial estate in grid square 6797.

**Function 2**

Communications centre – railway station at grid reference 658936.

**Function 3**

Health care – hospital at grid reference 624940.

**Function 4**

Administrative centre – county hall at grid reference 652923.

(c)  (i)  **Difference 1**

Some of the buildings and streets in areas X have open space between them, in contrast to area Y.

**Difference 2**

The streets in area Y are in a grid pattern; in area X they are irregular.

**Difference 3**

In area X there are many cul-de-sacs; in area Y there is only one.

(ii)  Area Y is nearer to the centre of Swansea than area X, which suggests that as the city expanded area Y was built first and at a later date area X was built. The layout of the streets in area Y is typical of terraced housing built in the 19th century, while the layout of area X is typical of an estate built within the last few decades.

(d)  (i)  The terraced houses have been demolished and replaced by a car park.

(ii)  The process that has taken place is called redevelopment.

(iii)  **Reason 1**

The transition zone is near the city centre and contains some of the oldest housing and industrial buildings which are often dirty, old fashioned and in need of repair. So they are relatively cheap to buy and planning permission is easy to get.

**Reason 2**

The area of the CBD is constantly looking to expand into the transition zone, providing the money for redevelopment.

(e)  **Chosen area – S**

Some of the buildings in the area are large (e.g. grid reference 655928); these could contain large department stores or an enclosed shopping centre. This, together with the bus or coach station, the information centre (grid reference 654928) and the museum just outside the area suggest that the area has a number of high-order services typical of the CBD.

The area contains the bus or coach station, and the railway station is on the edge of the ringed area at grid reference 658936. Also the A4067, the A4118, the A483, the A4067 and the A4217 either pass through the area or join each other within 0.5 kilometre of the edge of the ringed area. These facts suggest that the area is the centre of communications in Swansea and an area of high accessibility which is likely to attract the typical high-order services associated with the CBD.

The roads within the area mainly have dual carriageways which suggests that this is the area of highest traffic volume, another common feature of the CBD.

(c) **Answers to Multiple-choice and Completion Questions**

1 A
2 D
3 C
4 C
5 D

# 9 Development

## 9.1 Measuring development

### (a) Defining Development

The term 'development' implies that a process of change is operating which improves the quality of life of the population.

### (b) Levels of Development

1. Levels of development vary between and within countries of the world.
2. Economic and social indicators of development are used to try to decide the level of development of a country or region.

**Table 9.1** Some economic and social indicators of development

| Development indicators |
| --- |
| Population per doctor |
| Adult literacy (% of population) |
| Food intake in calories |
| Death rate per 1000 of population |
| Daily newspapers per 1000 of population |
| % of labour force in agriculture (see Table 11.4) |
| Gross national product per capita |
| Telephones per 1000 of population |
| Average life expectancy |

3. It is misleading to use a small number of indicators.
4. An increase in the **gross national product**, **GNP** (the total financial value of the goods and services provided in a country in a year) does not necessarily mean development for the population as a whole; the increased wealth may affect only a small percentage of the people.

# 9.2 Contrasts in development

### (a) The Pattern of Global Inequality

1. Using a range of economic and social indicators of development, the Brandt Report of 1980 divided the world into 'north' and 'south'.

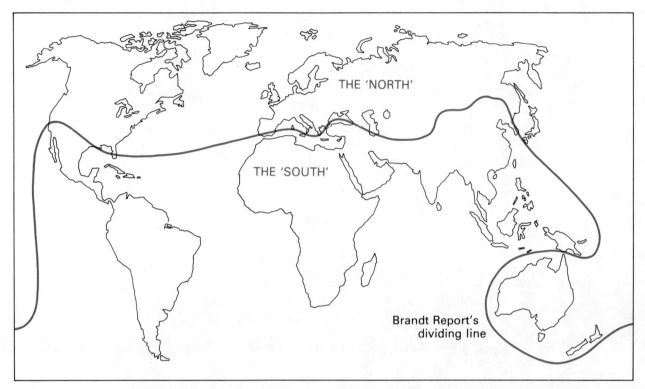

THE 'NORTH'

THE 'SOUTH'

Brandt Report's dividing line

**Figure 9.1**   The pattern of global inequality in levels of development

**Table 9.2**   The location of 'types' of country

| Type of economy | Location | Examples |
| --- | --- | --- |
| 1. Wealthy industrial market (capitalist) economies | 'North' | USA<br>Australia<br>West Germany |
| 2. Centrally planned (socialist) industrial economies | 'North' | USSR<br>Poland |
| 3. High-income oil exporting countries | 'South' | Saudi Arabia<br>Kuwait |
| 4. Middle-income economies | 'South' | Brazil<br>Ghana |
| 5. Low-income economies | 'South' | Mali<br>Ethiopia |

2. Types 1 and 2 (see Table 9.2) are found in the 'north' (the developed countries), the rest in the 'south' (the developing countries).
3. The gap in the level of development is widening.

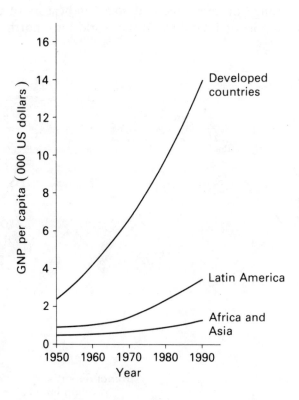

**Figure 9.2**  The development gap

## 9.3   Internal barriers to development

**(a) Internal Barriers**

1. Internal barriers result from the conditions in a particular country.
2. They hinder its development and as a result they maintain the in-equalities that exist between one country and another.

**Table 9.3**   Internal barriers to development

| Barrier | Explanation |
|---------|-------------|
| The environment | Many developing countries are in the tropics where the more delicately balanced ecosystems are more likely to be destroyed due to inappropriate farming methods, deforestation and population pressure. Also, natural hazards such as drought, earthquakes and hurricanes occur more frequently. |
| Population growth | The higher growth rate in developing countries means that any development that creates an increase in GNP has to be shared between an increasing number of people, so the overall quality of life of the population is harder to improve (see Section 7.2(b)). |

| | |
|---|---|
| Education and health | The lower levels of health and education services reduce the quality of life and hinder the formation of a labour force able to implement development strategies. |
| Government | Governments can hinder development by following policies that are racist or advantageous to the ruling elite. Unstable governments often spend money on defence and may become involved in war which is often responsible for a decline in the level of development. |
| Capital availability | Capital for development is in short supply because the low average earnings of the people of developing countries mean that individual savings and taxation are low. Both individuals and the economy are in a vicious circle which is difficult to break. |

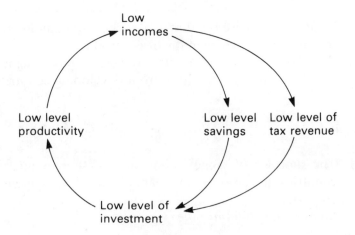

**Figure 9.3** The vicious circle of poverty

## 9.4 External barriers to development

### (a) External Barriers

1. External barriers result from the conditions outside a particular country.
2. They hinder its development and as a result they maintain the inequalities that exist between one country and another.

### (b) Colonialism

1. Many developing countries were colonised by European powers.
2. The main economic purpose of colonisation was to obtain a supply of raw materials to be manufactured in the 'home' country.
3. The main problems that this created for the developing countries were:

   (a) the introduction of cash crops at the expense of food crops to the extent that food crops have to be imported

(b) dependence on overseas markets

(c) the creation of transport networks designed to speed the export of raw materials rather than the development of the particular country

(d) raw materials were exported hindering the growth of manufacturing industry.

4. Today, although many colonies have gained their political independence, their affairs are still influenced by the developed countries through commerce and aid programmes. This dependence is called **neocolonialism**.

### (c) International Trade Restrictions

1. The present pattern of international trade works in favour of the developed countries.

2. For many developing countries the pattern of trade has remained unchanged since the end of colonialism. Their exports are mainly primary products and their imports are manufactured goods.

3. The difference between the value of primary products and manufactured goods has increased so that it takes a greater amount of primary products to buy a particular manufactured product.

4. The developed countries impose restrictions designed to protect their industries from competition from developing countries.

### (d) Capital

1. The shortage of money from internal sources means that developing countries have to obtain capital for development from developed countries.

2. Sources of capital include:

(a) voluntary aid organisations (e.g. Oxfam). Money is given where needed

(b) bilateral aid from one government to another. Money is in the form of a loan or a grant

(c) multilateral aid; developed countries pay money into international organisations (e.g. the World Bank) which is distributed to successful applicants in the form of a loan or grant

(d) companies, often multinational companies, invest in a developing country.

3. Borrowing money can hinder development, because often a large percentage of any growth in the GNP has to be used to pay the interest on the borrowed money and to repay the loan.

4. Where foreign aid is used solely to overcome a crisis (e.g. an earthquake) it can encourage complacency and does nothing to lessen the impact in the future of a similar crisis.

5. Bilateral aid is often tied so that the country receiving the aid has to spend it on agreed projects and its imports are mainly from the donor country.

6. Multinational companies often have limited impact on the development of the country as a whole because the bulk of the companies' earnings return to the 'home' country.

# 9.5  Theories of development

## (a)  The Core Periphery Model

1.  The core periphery model can be applied at the national and global scale. It recognises that there are core areas where the economy is more developed and growing and peripheral or outlying areas where development is less and growth is slower or not present.

2.  The periphery can contain a number of sub-areas:

    (a)  small growth areas
    (b)  declining regions
    (c)  resource–frontier regions which are being opened up often to extract raw materials.

3.  The effect of the core on the periphery is uncertain. Some people believe that the wealth of the core will 'trickle down' to the periphery and ensure that it develops. Others believe that the core will continue to develop at a faster rate than the periphery widening the gap between the two.

## (b)  Rostow's Model of Economic Growth

1.  Rostow believed that economic growth was dependent on the amount and type of industrial development in a country.
2.  As a country developed it would pass through five stages. Countries in stage 1 were not as developed as countries in stage 5.

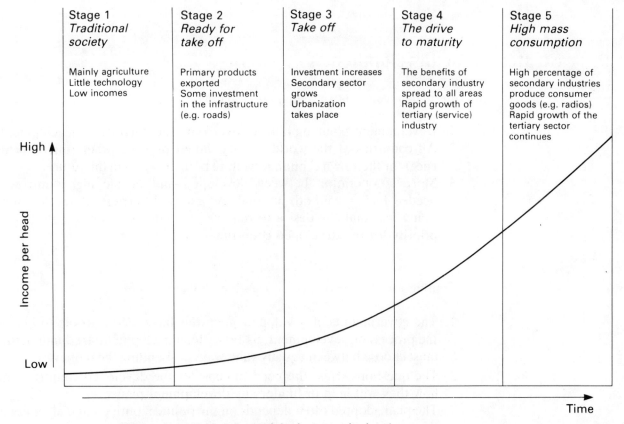

Figure 9.4  Rostow's model of economic development

3. Most of the developed countries have reached stages 4 or 5 while most of the developing countries are in stages 1, 2 or 3.
4. Some developing countries have adopted Rostow's ideas and tried to speed up development by rapid industrialisation (e.g. Brazil). This has had advantages and disadvantages.

**Table 9.4** Advantages and disadvantages of rapid industrialisation

| Advantages | Disadvantages |
| --- | --- |
| The economy is less dependent on agriculture which is reliant on the unpredictable weather and fluctuations in prices | Competes with the traditional craft industries |
| Reduces the amount of imports | Borrowed money creates international debt |
| Increases skill levels | Investment by foreign firms means that the profits go out of the country |
| Encourages the improvement of the infrastructure | Mechanisation needed to compete on the world market means that fewer jobs are created |
| Increases the GNP | Investment in industry means that investment in other sectors is reduced |
| Produces products to improve agriculture (e.g. fertiliser and farm machinery) | |

## 9.6 Strategies for development

### (a) Interdependence and Development Planning

1. Development planning aims to overcome the barriers to development.
2. All countries of the world are dependent on each other (**interdependence**) for their own economic welfare both now and in the future.
3. More co-operation between developed and developing countries is needed to remove both internal and external barriers to development. Many feel that the desire to remove inequalities is not a high enough priority for the developed countries.

### (b) Planning for Development in a Developing Country

1. The governments of developing countries have a crucial role to play in the process of development; as funds for development are limited, they must choose between equally valid ways of spending the money.
2. The questions stress the need to consider the developed countries and how they will help or hinder any development plan.
3. The plan adopted often depends on the political outlook and alliances of the government of the individual country.

**Figure 9.5** Some questions that governments of developing countries must answer

## 9.7 Inequalities in levels of development within a country

### (a) Causes of Inequality

1. Inequalities occur either when the wealth of a growth region is not spread to other regions and/or when a region is in decline.
2. Industrial decline is a common reason for the decline of a region.

### (b) Causes of Industrial Decline within a Region

1. Sometimes a region has a particular set of locational attractions for a limited range of primary and secondary industries.
2. This limited range of industry stimulates the development of the region as a result of the **multiplier effect** (see Figure 9.6).
3. These core industries may decline because of a variety of reasons (e.g. resource is exhausted).
4. Linked primary, secondary and tertiary industries also decline.
5. Once industrial decline has begun it becomes harder to attract new industry because the area becomes unattractive (see Figure 9.7).

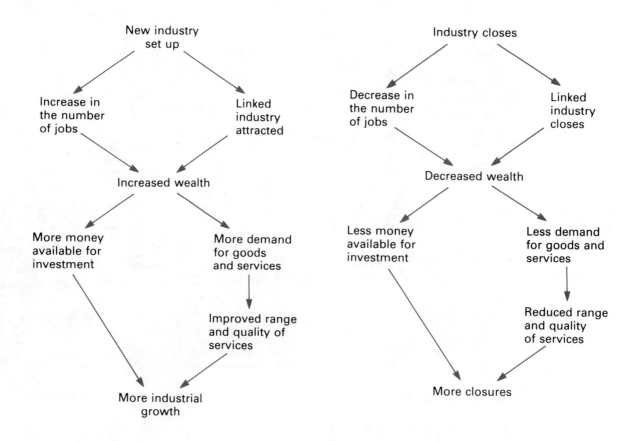

| New industry set up | Industry closes |

**Figure 9.6**   The multiplier effect                    **Figure 9.7**   The multiplier effect in reverse

### (c)  The Effects of Industrial Decline on a Region

**Table 9.5**   The effects of industrial decline on a region

| *Environmental problems* | *Social problems* |
|---|---|
| The problem of industrial pollution is often worse in declining regions because the industries in decline are the old traditional heavy industries which are characterised by large ugly buildings, a history of bad waste disposal which has left unsightly waste tips which can be toxic, and a high level of river pollution. | Unemployment is high in declining regions. The reduced income of the unemployed and the lack of job opportunities causes stress for individuals and families. The search for work may involve people leaving the area causing the break-up of families and neighbourhood communities. |

### (d)  Strategies for Regional Development within a Country

1. Strategies for regional development are usually associated with declining industrial regions.
2. Their aim is to attract new industrial development.
3. They are usually implemented by the national government.

**Table 9.6**   Solutions to industrial decline in a region

> 1. Recognition of areas of regional decline which need help from the government (e.g. enterprise zones).
> 2. Incentives to attract new and different industry to the area (e.g. tax relief, exemption from rates, freedom from some planning controls and the provision of buildings and services, often on industrial estates).
> 3. Re-training: often the skills of the workers made redundant are not the same as those needed for the new industry.
> 4. Government restrictions to prevent building in growth areas.
> 5. The decentralisation of government offices from the core areas to the areas of regional decline.
> 6. Improving the environment by refurbishing or redeveloping visually unattractive sites.
> 7. Mounting a publicity campaign to show the improvements and overcome the traditional image of a declining region.

## 9.8   Development examples

**Table 9.7**   Development examples

| Named examples of | Factual information needed | Your named example |
|---|---|---|
| 1. Countries of different types of economy (5 in all) | Name of country, type of economy, location ('north' or 'south'). Level of development of each measured by 3 or 4 development indicators. | 1.<br>2.<br>3.<br>4.<br>5. |
| 2. Country with internal barriers to development | Name of country, location, details of internal barriers. | 6. |
| 3. Country with external barriers to development | Name of country, location, details of external barriers. | 7. |
| 4. Country where modern, rapid industrial growth has been used to try to achieve a higher level of economic development | Name and location of country. Examples of industries developed (sketch map), with whose help. Benefits and problems that have occurred. | 8. |
| 5. Country where development plan has used intermediate technology with limited help from developed countries | Name and location of country. Examples of industrial and agricultural schemes that have been introduced. Benefits and problems caused. | 9. |

| | | |
|---|---|---|
| 6. Trade pattern of a developing country and a developed country | Goods that are imported and exported with percentage value. Destination of exports and origin of imports. Gains and losses as a result of trading pattern. Name and location of countries. | 10. 11. |
| 7. Country that gives aid | Name and location of country. How much aid is given and to whom. | 12. |
| 8. Country that receives aid | Name and location of country. How much aid is received from whom. | 13. |
| 9. Region that has suffered industrial decline | Name and location of region. Description of reasons for and effects of decline. | 14. |
| 10. Region that has received help from government | Name and location of region. Description of help given. Effects of help on region. | 15. |
| 11. Area that is an enterprise zone | Name and location of area. Details of changes as a result of enterprise zone status. | 16. |

## 9.9 Questions and answers

### (a) Multiple-choice and Completion Questions

1 The main feature of the 'green revolution' is the:

    **A** mechanisation of farming methods
    **B** increase in the amount of agricultural land
    **C** development of new strains of crops
    **D** spread of new ideas about conservation
    **E** banning of urban development on farm land.

                        (**NEA** syllabus A paper 1 question 6 1988)

2 Which of the following is sometimes an external barrier to development?

    **A** international trade
    **B** the environment
    **C** education levels
    **D** health levels
    **E** the national government

**3** Which of the following is not an effect of industrial decline?

    **A** unemployment
    **B** out-migration
    **C** derelict buildings
    **D** high average wages
    **E** pollution

**4** Which of the statements that are shown in the figure and written below are incorrect:

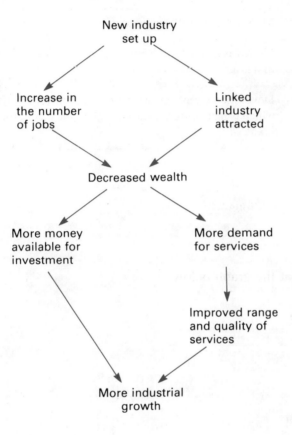

The multiplier effect

    **A** linked industry attracted
    **B** decreased wealth
    **C** less money available for investment
    **D** more demand for services
    **E** more industrial growth

**5** Complete the table below by putting the correct term opposite the definition that it applies to:

Terms: bilateral aid
        multilateral aid
        voluntary aid

Types of aid

| Type of aid | Description |
|---|---|
| | Money is given where needed |
| | Money is given by one government to another in the form of a loan or a grant |
| | Developed countries pay money into international organisations which is distributed to successful applicants in the form of a loan or grant |

### (b) Structured Questions

### Example 9.1

(a) Look at the graph below:

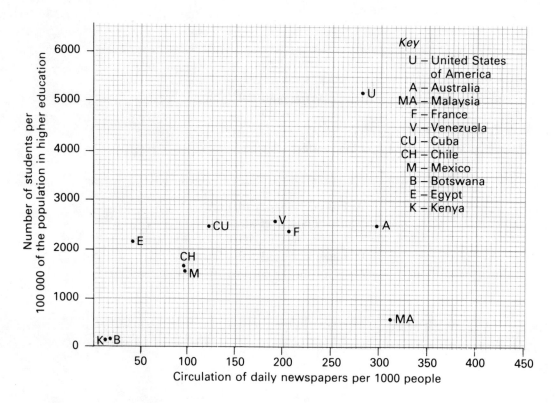

Scatter graph showing the number of students per 100 000 of the population in higher education and the circulation of daily newspapers per 1000 people for selected countries

132

(i) Add the countries of Canada and Senegal to the graph using the values below:

Statistics for Senegal and Canada

|  | Senegal | Canada |
|---|---|---|
| Number of students per 100 000 of the population in higher education | 206 | 5090 |
| Circulation of daily newspapers per 1000 people | 5 | 220 |

(ii) State which of the following general statements are true and which are false:

**Statement 1**
As the number of people in higher education goes up so does the circulation of daily newspapers.
**Statement 2**
As the number of people in higher education and the circulation of daily newspapers increase the level of development of a country decreases.

(iii) Using the graph put the following countries in rank order of development:

USA Senegal France Chile

(b) (i) Give two reasons why the number of people in higher education can be used to help decide the level of development of a country.
(ii) Explain why it would be difficult to decide whether Malaysia was more or less developed than Cuba if you were using only the graph.
(iii) List three other sets of information you would want to use to decide if Malaysia was more or less developed than Cuba.

(c) Look at the figure below:

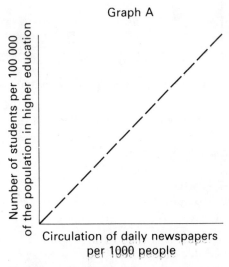

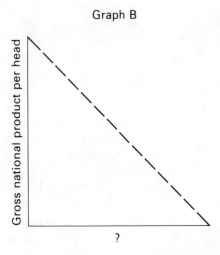

Two best-fit lines

133

(i) The best-fit line on graph A summarises the relationship shown by the scatter graph. Complete graph B by adding a title, chosen from the list below, to the blank axis:

percentage employed in agriculture
number of washing machines per head
average calorie intake per head

(ii) Explain your choice in (c) (i).
(iii) Give a reason why GNP per head can be a misleading guide to the level of development in a country.

(d) Name an example of a developing country. Briefly describe the modern industrial developments that have taken place in the secondary sector of the economy and explain any problems they have created.

**Solution 9.1**

(a)  (i) See the figure below:

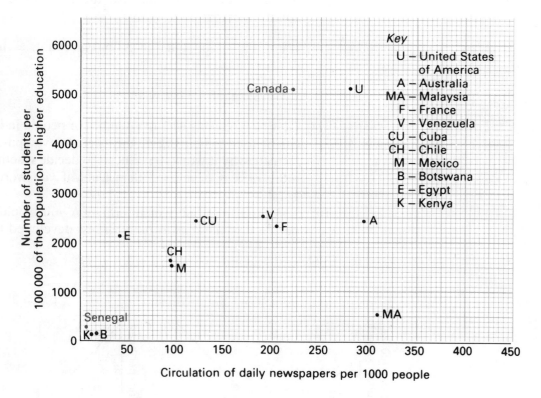

Scatter graph showing the number of students per 100 000 of the population in higher education and the circulation of daily newspapers per 1000 people for selected countries

(ii) Statement 1 is true.
Statement 2 is false.
(iii) Rank 1 – USA.
Rank 2 – France.
Rank 3 – Chile.
Rank 4 – Senegal.

(b)  (i) **Reason 1**
The quality of life of individuals is higher in a country where they have an increased chance of entering higher education, if they so wish.
**Reason 2**
The ability of individuals and/or governments to pay for higher education depends on the wealth of the country. In general increased wealth means a higher percentage in further education.

(ii) It is difficult to decide whether Malaysia is more developed than Cuba because the graph shows only two measures of development. Cuba has more students per 100 000 of the population while Malaysia has a greater circulation of daily newspapers per 1000 of the population. It is impossible to say which of the measures indicates the higher level of development.

(iii) The other information that I would want:

1. the percentage of people employed in different sectors of the economy
2. the gross national product
3. the number of doctors per head of population.

(c)  (i) The correct label for the blank axis is the percentage employed in agriculture.

(ii) In general as GNP increases the employment structure of a country changes; a higher percentage of people work in the secondary and tertiary sectors and a lower percentage in agriculture. This is because an increase in GNP makes more money available to invest and spend in the secondary and tertiary sectors, which grow, employing more people and producing goods (e.g. tractors) that reduce the need for agricultural workers.

(iii) The GNP per head does not indicate how the wealth of a country is distributed. It may be that a small percentage of the population hold most of the wealth and the remainder have a poor quality of life.

(d) **Named example – Brazil**
Since the 1940s the government of Brazil has invested in the development of secondary industry. Three types of industry have been developed: industries that make products that used to be imported (e.g. tractors at Campinas), industries that produce simple goods for the home market (e.g. shoes and cement) and industries that encourage the growth of other linked industries (e.g. steel at Volta Redonda). Multinational companies (e.g. Ford) were encouraged to help these developments because of their finance and technological skills.

The problems associated with the development are the uneven distribution of wealth and the dependence on the world market and multinationals.

The higher wages paid by the secondary sector (whilst low compared with those in a 'western' country) have increased the wealth gap between the rural and urban dwellers and between the south east where most of the development has been concentrated and the rest of the country. The industrial development has involved high capital investment in machinery creating less employment in rural areas than if intermediate technology had been introduced. The higher wages have also stimulated rural-to-urban migration; often the migrants have not been able to find jobs and have been forced to live in 'favelas'.

The industrial development has been financed by borrowing; repayments and interest payments have meant that the profits of industrialisation have been reduced; and where multinationals are concerned the profits have been taken·out of the country. The recession of the 1980s reduced the sales and profits of Brazil's industry, making it impossible to meet interest payments on loans. The recession also meant that multinational companies had to cut back their operations (e.g. Massey Ferguson reduced output at its tractor factory).

**Example 9.2**

(a) Look at the figure below:

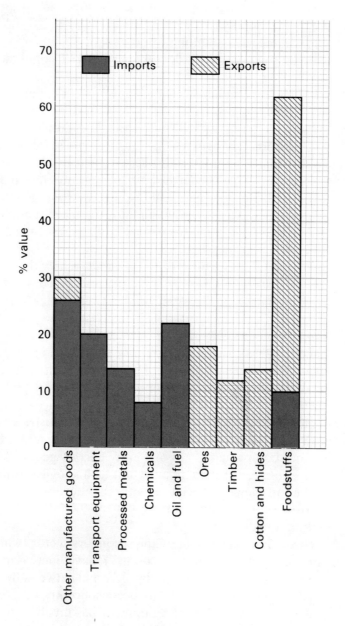

The percentage value of items imported and exported by country X, a 'typical' developing country

(i) What percentage of the country's imports by value is oil and fuel?
(ii) List the items that are imported but not exported.
(iii) What percentage of the country's exports are products of second-ary industry?
(iv) Why is the pattern of trade typical of developing countries?

(b) Look at the figure below:

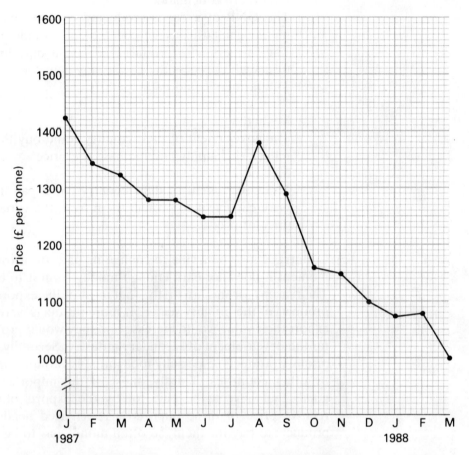

The price of cocoa on the first of the month between January 1987 and March 1988

(i) Describe the trend shown by the graph.
(ii) Give a possible reason for the trend in cocoa prices.
(iii) What will be the effect of the trend on the GNP of a country that produces cocoa?
(iv) Give one group of people who may gain from the trend and one group who will lose.
(v) Suggest two methods that could be used to help the group who are losing.

(c) Use the two figures above and any other information that you have to explain why country X may be trying to change its pattern of trade.

**Solution 9.2**

(a)   (i) 22%
     (ii) Transport equipment, processed metals, chemicals and oil and fuel.
     (iii) 4%.

(iv) The pattern of trade is typical of developing countries because a high percentage of the country's exports are primary products and a high percentage of imports are manufactured goods.

(b) (i) The trend on the graph is downward, the price of cocoa per tonne falling from £1425 in January 1987 to £1000 in March 1988.

(ii) A good harvest has meant that there is a greater supply of cocoa than there is demand.

(iii) The GNP of a cocoa-producing country may fall because the money gained from the cocoa crop has fallen.

(iv) The farmers who produce the cocoa may lose. The manufacturers who process the cocoa may gain.

(v) The farmers could be helped by:

**Method 1**
The government of their country could buy the surplus cocoa to reduce the supply and increase the price.
**Method 2**
The government of their country could pay the farmers a fixed price each year to protect them from the variations in the world price of cocoa.

(c) Country X may be trying to change its pattern of trade because at the moment it does not earn enough money from it to help development. The reasons for this are firstly, that most of the exports are unprocessed products of the primary sector. If more products were processed before export their value would increase and they would provide raw materials for the development of secondary industry. Secondly, the price of these primary products, especially foodstuffs, is variable and often controlled by other countries. Thirdly, most of the imports are manufactured goods that have to be paid for by the exports of the country. The relative price of these imports has increased needing more primary products to pay for them, so often money has to be borrowed.

(c) **Answers to Multiple-choice and Completion Questions**

1 C
2 A
3 D
4 C
5 See the figure below:

Types of aid

| Type of aid | Description |
|---|---|
| Voluntary | Money is given where needed |
| Bilateral | Money is given by one government to another in the form of a loan or a grant |
| Multi-lateral | Developed countries pay money into international organisations which is distributed to successful applicants in the form of a loan or grant |

# 10 Transport

## 10.1  Characteristics and measurement of transport networks

### (a) Nodes and Links

1. A transport network (e.g. the road network) is made up of **nodes** at the end of a route or where two routes join, and **links** which join together the nodes.
2. Different networks often have the same nodes allowing people and goods to transfer from one network to another.
3. A network can be shown as a **topological map** where the links are shown as straight lines with no indication of distance.

### (b) Density

1. This is the number of links per unit area (e.g. square kilometre).
2. The network is usually denser where population density is high, the size of the country is small and/or the country is developed.

### (c) Connectivity

Connectivity is the amount of connection between nodes in a network and is measured by the **beta index**.

$$\frac{\text{Number of links}}{\text{Number of nodes}} = \text{Beta index}$$

EXAMPLE A

Beta index = 0.8

A beta index of less than 1 represents a **branching network** where connectivity is low

EXAMPLE B

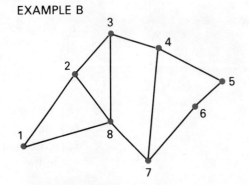

Beta index = 1.4

A beta index of greater than 1 represents a **complete** or **circuit network** where connectivity is high

**Figure 10.1**  The beta index: branching and circuit networks

**(d) Accessibility**

1. **Accessibility**, the ease with which people can reach a place, varies from place to place.
2. The variations in the accessibility of places in a network can be summarised by an accessibility matrix.
3. To find this index for a place add up the number of links that a person must travel over to reach each of the other places in the network. A complete matrix does this for all the places in the network.

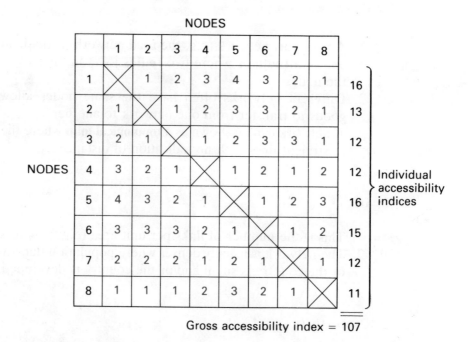

The node with the lowest accessibility index is the most accessible (i.e. node 8)

The **gross accessibility index** is found by adding up the individual accessibility indices (i.e. 107)

**Figure 10.2**  An accessibility matrix for example B in Figure 10.1

4. The accessibility index is a crude measure because accessibility is not only affected by the number of links between places.
5. Distance between places can be measured in a number of ways:

   (a) linear distance, the number of kilometres
   (b) time distance, the time that the journey takes
   (c) cost distance, the cost of the journey which is related to distance and time.

6. A place which is quicker and/or cheaper to reach, usually because the distance is less, is said to be more accessible.
7. An individual's perception of distance, journey time and cost may be wrong, so they do not visit the most accessible place to obtain what they require.

### (e) Detours

1. The **detour index** compares the straight-line distance between two places with the actual measured distance.

$$\frac{\text{Measured distance along a link}}{\text{Straight-line distance}} \times 100 = \text{Detour index}$$

The higher the number above 100 the greater the detour

**Figure 10.3** The detour index

2. Detours are made to avoid obstacles which would be difficult and costly to overcome (e.g. estuaries can be bridged).
3. The decision makers have to consider the costs and benefits of the detour and the straight-line route. The latter will usually be more expensive to build but cheaper to use once built.
4. Building technology has improved so that more physical obstacles can be overcome. It follows that older routes are more liable to have longer detours.

## 10.2 Flows along networks

### (a) Flow Patterns

1. Flows or movement within a network group together to form patterns.
2. These patterns have peaks when many flows are taking place (e.g. commuting to work) and troughs when few flows are taking place.
3. Most flows are over short distances because **distance decay** is operating (as distance increases the number of people travelling the longer distance decreases).

### (b) Estimating Flows

1. The **gravity model** uses the population size and the distance between two places to calculate the volume of flows between them.

$$\text{Volume of movement between places A and B} = \frac{\text{Population of place A} \times \text{Population of place B}}{(\text{Distance between A and B})^2}$$

**Figure 10.4** The gravity model

2. The prediction of flows between two places is important if any increase is to be planned.

141

# 10.3 Modes of transport

### (a) Competition between Modes

1. **Modes** or types of transport compete with each other to move goods and people.
2. Where a choice of mode is available the user has to consider the following factors which will decide the cost of the journey and the mode that is chosen:

   (a) the speed and comfort required
   (b) the type, amount and weight of the goods or people to be moved
   (c) the number of times loading and unloading will take place
   (d) the distance.

3. Sometimes a mode has such an advantage over other modes for a type of user and journey (e.g. tourists to Spain from the UK usually travel by air) that competition between modes is at a minimum.
4. Where this is not the case competition between modes for the same users is strong.
5. Competition encourages the search for more efficient vehicles, networks and handling facilities. The technological development of one network makes it more competitive.

### (b) Advantages of Modes for Freight Transport

Table 10.1 The advantages of different modes for freight transport

| Mode | Cost per tonne km | Speed | Flexibility | Most competitive for |
|------|-------------------|-------|-------------|----------------------|
| Air | High: decreases greatly with distance | Fast | Airports only | Low-bulk high-value goods that need to be moved quickly over sea and/or land |
| Road | Medium: almost constant as distance increases | Medium | Most settlements | Low to medium bulks of all values on short and medium journeys over land (especially when more than one drop-off is needed) |
| Rail | Medium: decreases with distance | Medium/ fast | Settlements with stations | All bulks and values over medium and long distances on land quickly |
| Water (ship/ barge) | Low: decreases with distance | Slow | River and sea ports only | High-bulk low-value goods over water that do not need quick movement |
| Pipeline | Low: constant with increased distance | Continuous | Start and end. Over land and under water | High volume of liquids of any value where demand is likely to be continuous for a long time |

**(c) Advantages of Modes for Passenger Transport**

**Table 10.2** Advantages of different modes for passenger transport

| Mode | People and journeys for which the mode is most competitive |
|------|------------------------------------------------------------|
| Air | Long distances where speed rather than cost is important. |
| Car | Short distances on normal roads and medium distances on motorways where it is convenient to have a flexible start and finish time and where the destination is not served by another mode. |
| Bus | Short and medium distances where the cost of travel needs to be low and the stress of driving avoided; where the start and end of the journey are near a station and the timetable is convenient. |
| Train | Medium and long distances where comfort and the avoidance of stress are important; where the start and end of the journey are near a station and the timetable is convenient. |

## 10.4 The growth and decline of transport networks

**(a) Causes and Effects of the Growth and Decline of Transport Networks**

1. Economic activities require efficient transport networks to allow access to their raw materials, markets and labour force.
2. Both growth and decline of networks change the relative accessibility of places making some more accessible than they used to be and others less accessible.
3. Growth can result in the building of a new link between two places that already have a link or to a place that was previously not part of the network. Decline can lead to the removal of a link.

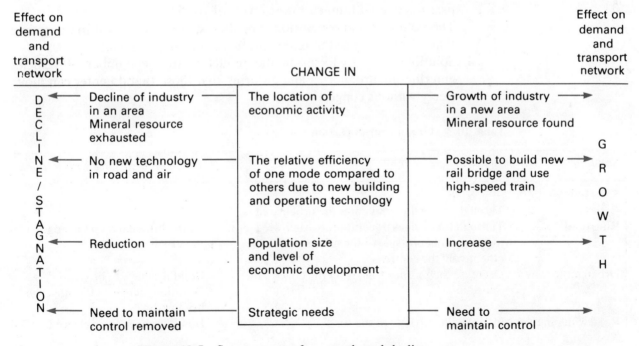

**Figure 10.5** Some reasons for growth and decline

143

### (b) Transport Growth and Economic Development

1. Transport networks in developed countries are denser than those in developing countries because the higher level of economic development and activity in the former creates a greater demand for the movement of goods and people.
2. A transport network may also grow when the construction of a new link is seen as a way to stimulate economic development by allowing the import and export of raw materials and finished products and the spread of education and health care to a previously isolated area.

## 10.5 Transport problems: causes and solutions

### (a) Urban and Rural Areas

1. The demand for transport is increasing and causing congestion, a greater risk of pollution and accidents to motorists and pedestrians.
2. A planning solution is to build a new terminus or a new link.
3. While the majority recognise the need for the development, the choice of route or location causes conflict. Those people who live near the proposed development often object because the development will reduce their quality of life by creating additional noise, air and visual pollution and will use land which may be of particular beauty or agricultural value.

### (b) Urban Areas

1. Urban areas are important nodes on transport networks that attract large numbers of travellers, especially when people are moving to and from work.
2. Many of these urban areas have a road network that was designed in the past to cope with much lower levels of traffic.
3. The pollution and congestion, together with the increased journey time that is created, are the major problems facing planners.
4. Solutions tend to focus on the reduction of the number of vehicles entering the urban area and ensuring that those that do enter can move freely without congestion.

**Table 10.3** Urban transport solutions

| Solution | Desired effect | Problems associated with solution |
|---|---|---|
| **Road building** | | |
| Bypass | Through traffic does not enter the urban area | |
| Ring road | Through traffic does not enter the urban area and journeys from one side of the urban area to the other avoid the centre | Agricultural land on the edge of the urban area is lost |
| Urban motorway | Decrease the journey time from the edge to the centre | Buildings have to be cleared Pollution increased for those who live nearby |
| Road widening | Increase the capacity of the road | Buildings have to be cleared |

| Public transport | | |
|---|---|---|
| Bus lanes | Reduce journey time making buses a better alternative to cars | |
| Park and ride | Reduce number of cars entering the urban area by providing alternative | Providing an efficient service for the increased numbers |
| Cut charges | Free public transport encourages its use | |
| **Parking** | | |
| Multi-storey | Save space and reduce congestion caused by on-street parking | |
| Raise charges | Discourage cars from entering | Increases cost of journey |
| Restrictions | Reduce congestion and discourage cars from entering | Creates extra movement as people look for a parking space |
| **Others** | | |
| One-way system | Increase speed of movement | Lengthens journey |
| Tidal flow | Increases capacity of road at peak times | |
| Precincts | Reduce danger to pedestrians | Increases length of journey |

5. These solutions are often used together to try to solve the urban transport problem.

## (c) Rural Areas

1. The increased use of private transport in developed countries has reduced the demand for public transport. In order to avoid heavy losses public transport companies have reduced the frequency of the service and cut down the number of routes that they use.
2. Some sections of the rural community still need to use public transport but because of the decline in the service they have become increasingly isolated.
3. In developing countries the problem in rural areas is not a decline in services but a lack of services because of the lack of demand and funds to provide a service.
4. Multi-purpose vehicles designed to carry both freight and people are used in both types of country to reduce the costs of providing the service and ensuring that money is not wasted.
5. In developed countries subsidies are sometimes given to companies that maintain unprofitable rural services. Self-help schemes which share the use of cars and minibuses are another solution.

## 10.6 Transport examples

**Table 10.4** Transport examples

| Named examples of | Factual information needed | Your named example |
|---|---|---|
| 1. Branching network | Location and reasons for network type. Effect on economic and social activity. | 1. |
| 2. Circuit network | Location and reasons for network type. Effect on economic and social activity. | 2. |
| 3. An urban area | Location. Peaks and troughs of traffic flows in 24-hour period. Reasons for journeys. Effects of peaks. Problems and solutions of traffic. | 3. |
| 4. A rural area | Location. Problems and solutions of traffic. | 4. |
| 5. A network that is growing due to increased demand | Location. Reasons for growth. Effects of growth on accessibility. Conflict that results from choice of route and building of link. | 5. |
| 6. A network that is growing to try to stimulate development | Location. Effect of growth on accessibility and development. | 6. |
| 7. A network that is declining | Reasons for decline. Effects of decline on accessibility. Conflict that results from decline. | 7. |
| 8. Modes that have improved their operating technology | Description of improvement and the effect of the improvement on competition with other modes. | 8. |
| 9. Improvement in building technology to overcome physical obstacle | Location, description of improvement and effects. | 9. |
| 10. Network and mode in developing and developed countries | Description and explanation of differences. | 10. |
| 11. Airport | Location, sketch map of area. Conflict that has resulted. | 11. |
| 12. Port | Location, sketch map, description of the type of trade, trading area and handling facilities. | 12. |

# 10.7  Questions and answers

## (a)  Multiple-choice and Completion Questions

**1** Complete the accessibility matrix below:

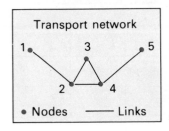

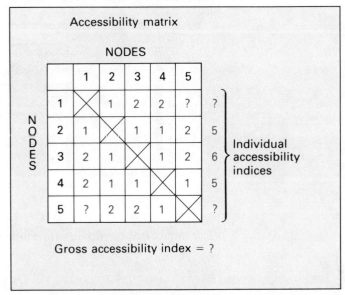

Accessibility matrix

**2** Which of the statements about road transport below is incorrect?

   **A** Road transport is slower than air and rail transport over long distances.
   **B** Road transport is the best mode for moving high-bulk, low-value goods.
   **C** Road congestion encourages travellers to use other modes.
   **D** Road transport is more accessible than other modes of transport.
   **E** Road transport is most competitive over medium and short distances.

**3** Which of the following is least likely to cause the growth of a transport network?

   **A** the discovery of a new mineral resource
   **B** an increase in the level of development
   **C** a stable population size
   **D** the construction of a new town
   **E** an improvement in bridge-building technology

**4** Complete the graph below:

| Time (a.m.) | 08.00 | 08.30 | 09.00 | 09.30 | 10.00 | 10.30 |
|---|---|---|---|---|---|---|
| Total number of cars travelling in previous half-hour | 245 | 220 | 150 | 90 | 75 | 90 |

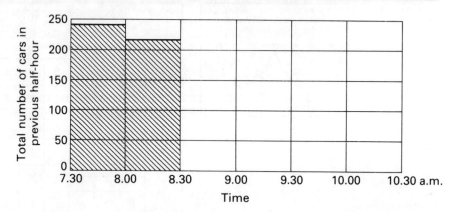

The number of car drivers travelling to work in London from Harlow

(**LEAG** syllabus A question b 27 specimen paper)

**5** For this question one or more of the responses given are correct. Decide which of the responses is (are) correct. Then choose:

**A** if 1, 2 and 3 are all correct
**B** if 1 and 2 only are correct
**C** if 2 and 3 only are correct
**D** if 1 only is correct
**E** if 3 only is correct.

Which of the following are true statements about the problem of rural transport?

1. The decline of rural transport has caused equal hardship for all sections of the rural community.
2. The frequency of public transport services has decreased in many rural areas of the developed world.
3. Multi-purpose vehicles are one solution to the rural transport problem.

## (b) Structured Questions

### Example 10.1

(a) Look at the map below:

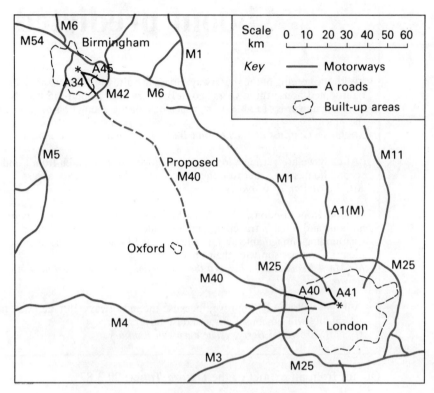

Part of the motorway network of southern England

(i) Describe the route of the proposed M40 motorway.
(ii) How will the accessibility of Oxford be changed by the new motorway?
(iii) Complete the table below:

Distances from London to Birmingham

| | |
|---|---|
| Distance in kilometres from London to Birmingham via the A40, the M40, the proposed M40 and the A34 | |
| Distance in kilometres from London to Birmingham via the A41, the M1, the M6, the M42 and the A45 | |

*Note:* the centre of both cities is marked *

(iv) Suggest and explain one reason why the new motorway may reduce journey times from Birmingham to London.

(b) Look at the figure below:

Quotes from an extract of the *Oxford Times*, 20.3.87

    (i) Describe the effect that the new motorway will have on house prices.

    (ii) What are the advantages of the area that are attracting house buyers from London?

    (iii) Suggest and explain two reasons why the village residents might object to people from outside the area buying houses in their village.

(c) Explain why a person working in the centre of a large city might choose to live in a rural area and commute to work each day rather than live in the suburbs of the city.

(d) Choose a named example of a transport development that has been completed and describe its harmful effects on the people who live nearby.

**Solution 10.1**

(a)    (i) The proposed route of the M40 continues the existing M40 from the south-east of Oxford and runs in a north-easterly direction to join the M42 to the south of Birmingham.

    (ii) The new motorway will increase the accessibility of Oxford by reducing the journey time between Birmingham and Oxford.

(iii) See the table below:

Distances from London to Birmingham

| Distance in kilometres from London to Birmingham via the A40, the M40, the proposed M40 and the A34 | *190 Km* |
|---|---|
| Distance in kilometres from London to Birmingham via the A41, the M1, the M6, the M42 and the A45 | *190 Km* |

(iv) The new motorway will reduce journey times between Birmingham and London by providing an additional motorway link. Delays due to traffic congestion on the M1 will be reduced as the volume of traffic will be split between the two motorways.

(b) (i) The new motorway will increase house prices enormously; already a one-bedroomed house in Banbury has increased by £19 000 in the last three years.

(ii) The area has cheaper houses than the London area. The area will be only one and a half hour's travelling time from London. The area has desirable villages set in beautiful surroundings.

(iii) **Reason 1**
The residents of the village might object if they are first-time buyers because they cannot afford to pay the higher house prices that have resulted from the increased demand, as people from outside the area try to buy.
**Reason 2**
They may also object if the houses of the village are used as second homes, because as they will not always be occupied the services in the village may suffer from a loss of trade, which may force them to close down. The original residents will then have to travel further to obtain their services.

(c) A person who makes this choice has considered the advantages and disadvantages of living in a rural area rather than in the suburbs and decided that their quality of life will be improved if they live in the former.

A rural area offers an environment which has less noise, air and visual pollution, more open space and better facilities for and access to certain leisure activities (e.g. walking and cycling) than the suburbs of a city. House prices and services are generally cheaper than in the suburbs.

A suburban location is closer to the city centre reducing the cost and time of the journey to work. It has better access to certain high-order shopping facilities and certain types of leisure facilities (e.g. the theatre and cinema) than a rural area.

(d) **Named example of completed development – Heathrow airport**
Heathrow airport is the largest in the world and handles more than 27 million passengers each year. People who live nearby in Twickenham

and Staines, and especially those who live beneath the flight paths in Hounslow, Egham and Heston are affected by the noise and air pollution as the jets take off and land.

Double glazing and sound insulation, paid for by the airport authority reduce the noise inside the house, but only if the windows are closed. The continual take-offs (every thirty seconds at the busiest times) during day and night creates health problems for many people, and the fear of an aircraft crashing in a built-up area is a constant worry. These problems lower the house prices making it harder for the residents to move away.

**Example 10.2**

(a) Look at the information below:

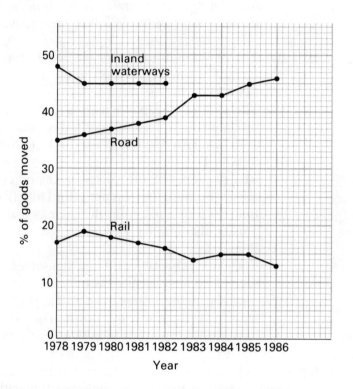

| | 1983 | 1984 | 1985 | 1986 |
|---|---|---|---|---|
| Percentage of goods moved by inland waterways | 43 | 42 | 40 | 41 |

The percentage of goods moved by different modes within the EEC

(i) Complete the graph by adding the percentages for the movement of goods by inland waterways.
(ii) Which method of transport moved the most freight in 1981?
(iii) Describe the trend of the movement of goods by the railways.
(iv) Use the graph to describe how competition between the modes has changed the percentage of goods that they carry.

(v) Complete the table below, by putting each of the phrases in the correct place:

**Phrase A**
Medium and high bulks of all values over medium and long distances quickly
**Phrase B**
High-bulk low-value goods that do not need quick movement
**Phrase C**
Low to medium bulks of all values on short and medium journeys (especially when more than one drop-off is needed)

Competition between modes for freight transport

| Mode | Most competitive for |
|---|---|
| Road | Phrase? |
| Rail | Phrase? |
| Water (ship/barge) | Phrase? |

(b) Look at the information below:

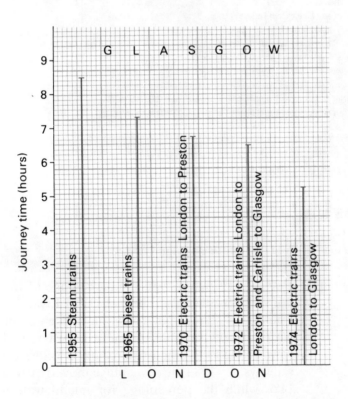

The effect of technological developments on journey times by rail from London to Glasgow

(i) Use the diagram to show how improvements in the technology used by the railways has increased the efficiency of the service.
(ii) Explain the advantages for a person travelling from London to Glasgow by train rather than by driving a car.

153

(c) Describe the British Rail offer shown below. Suggest and explain reasons why British Rail have made the offer.

British Rail advertisement

**Solution 10.2**

(a)  (i) See the figure on page 155.

(ii) Inland waterways.

(iii) Between 1978 and 1986 the percentage of freight moved by the railways has decreased from 17% to 13%.

(iv) The graph shows that roads have been competing successfully with both railways and inland waterways. In 1978 inland waterways carried the highest percentage followed by roads and then railways. By 1986 the percentage moved by road had increased by 11% while the percentage for inland waterways and railways decreased by 7% and 4% respectively. By 1986 roads carried the highest percentage of freight followed by inland waterways and then railways.

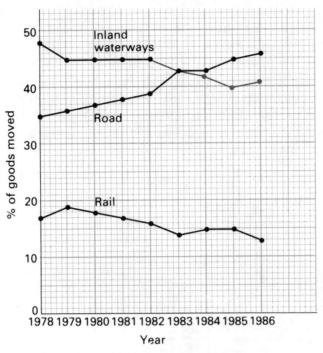

The percentage of goods moved by different modes within the EEC

(v) See the table below:

Competition between modes for freight transport

| Mode | Most competitive for |
|------|---------------------|
| Road | Phrase **C** |
| Rail | Phrase **A** |
| Water (ship/barge) | Phrase **B** |

(b) (i) The diagram shows that the change from steam to diesel engines and the gradual introduction of electrification between 1970 and 1974 increased the efficiency of the service by reducing the journey time from London to Glasgow by 3 hours 15 minutes.

(ii) Generally the journey is quicker by train than by car; it is more reliable as a car is more likely to be held up in congestion. The train is more comfortable as it is possible to walk round and stretch out; a car driver has to stop to do this, adding to the journey time. The train passenger can choose to relax or work during the journey while the car driver has to concentrate to avoid accidents.

(c) The British Rail offer is allowing senior citizens who hold a Senior Citizen Railcard to travel between any two stations for either £5 or £10 in the month of November. The offer does not apply on Fridays and weekday travel to London if the train arrives before 10 a.m.

The reasons for the offer are to try to increase the number of passengers who travel by rail at off-peak times. British Rail hope that partly empty trains can be filled, increasing the income from a scheduled journey at no extra cost. The offer is not available at peak times because the trains at these times are already full and any more passengers would reduce the quality of the service.

The price reductions in November are to persuade senior citizens to buy a railcard which it is hoped will increase demand for travel throughout the year; once a £12 card has been paid for it is more likely to be used again. The month of November has probably been chosen as this is a time of low demand for travel, as people save for the Christmas holiday.

**(c) Answers to Multiple-choice and Completion Questions**

**1** See the figure below:

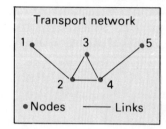

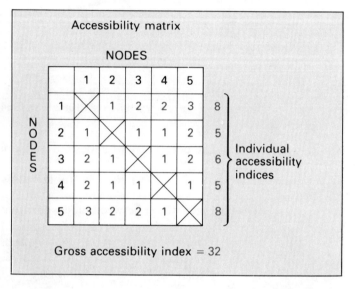

Accessibility matrix

**2 B**

**3 C**

**4** See the figure below:

| Time (a.m.) | 08.00 | 08.30 | 09.00 | 09.30 | 10.00 | 10.30 |
|---|---|---|---|---|---|---|
| Total number of cars travelling in previous half-hour | 245 | 220 | 150 | 90 | 75 | 90 |

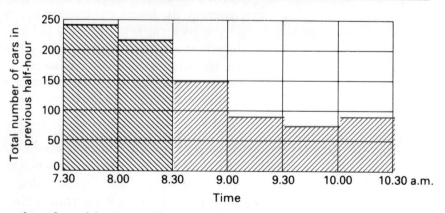

The number of car drivers travelling to work in London from Harlow

**5 C**

# 11 Agriculture

## 11.1 Agriculture as a system

### (a) The Components of the Agricultural System

1. Agriculture is a **primary** industry concerned with obtaining raw materials from the ground for immediate consumption or for processing.
2. All types of agriculture can be viewed as a system with inputs and outputs to and from the farm and processes occurring on the farm.
3. Outputs are the result of processes acting on the inputs.

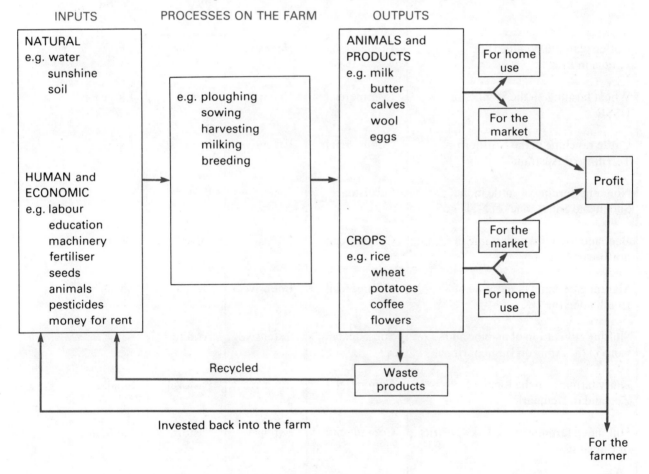

**Figure 11.1**  The agricultural system

### (b) Types of Agricultural System

1. Agricultural systems that have high inputs of capital and/or labour per unit of land are said to be **intensive**. **Extensive** systems have a low input of capital and labour per unit of land.

2. The types of output from the system vary:

   (a) Arable systems produce crops.
   (b) Pastoral systems produce animals.
   (c) Mixed systems produce both crops and animals.

3. The markets for the outputs vary:

   (a) Commercial systems produce crops and animals for sale.
   (b) Subsistence systems produce crops and animals to be consumed by the people who have grown them.

### (c) Example of Farming Types

**Table 11.1** Examples of different farming systems

| Example | Commercial/ subsistence | Intensive/ extensive | Arable/ pastoral/ mixed | Farm size small <25 ha medium 25–300 ha large >300 ha |
|---|---|---|---|---|
| Coffee plantation in the state of Parana in Brazil | Commercial | Intensive | Arable | Large |
| Wheat farming on the Steppes of the USSR | Commercial | Extensive | Arable | Large |
| Cattle ranching in the Northern Territory of Australia | Commercial | Extensive | Pastoral | Large |
| Nomadic herding of cattle in the Sudan and Sahel zones of Mali | Subsistence | Extensive | Pastoral | – |
| Beef and fodder crop farming in north-east England | Commercial | Intensive | Mixed | Medium |
| Market gardening in the Vale of Evesham in the UK | Commercial | Intensive | Arable | Small |
| Shifting cultivation of manioc and yams in the Amazon Basin of Brazil | Subsistence | Extensive | Arable | – |
| Dairy farming on the island of Zeeland in Denmark | Commercial | Intensive | Pastoral | Small |
| Hill sheep farming in the Lake District of England | Commercial | Extensive | Pastoral | Medium |
| Rice farming in the Ganges Valley in India | Subsistence | Intensive | Arable | Small |

## 11.2 The decision-making process

### (a) The Decision-making Process

1. The type of agricultural system that develops is a result of the decision-making process.
2. The farmer has to choose the crops and livestock that are to be produced.
3. The choice is limited by physical (e.g. climate), social (e.g. farm tenure), political (e.g. grants), and economic (e.g. market price) controls.
4. These controls vary from place to place and therefore so does the land use.

### (b) Individual Differences

1. Even if two farmers are limited by an identical set of controls they may not use the land in the same way.
2. They may perceive differently the controls under which they operate because of their different personalities.
3. They may perceive the risks differently (e.g. one farmer may be willing to risk growing the most profitable crop even though there is a greater risk of crop failure)..

### (c) Change and the Decision-making Process

1. The nature of agriculture in an area has developed over a period of time as a result of changes in the controls on the decision-making process; it will continue to change in response to changes in the controls.
2. The main reason for change is the desire to increase production and profit, by using more efficient methods, or by increasing the amount of land that is cultivated, or by changing the crops that are grown to meet new demand.
3. Change within the agricultural system can cause problems which result in less production and profit.

## 11.3 Physical controls on the decision-making process

### (a) Controls on the Choice of Crop

1. Each type of animal and crop has a set of physical requirements (e.g. wheat needs 800–1000 mm of rainfall etc.). If these requirements are not met by the area where the farm is situated then the particular crop or animal will not usually be produced.

**Figure 11.2** Physical controls on the decision-making process

2. Within these requirements each crop or animal has a set of conditions which are the **optimum** or best conditions which will produce the highest **yield** (amount of produce per hectare).

3. If production takes place away from the area where the optimum conditions are found yields will decrease unless more money is invested to overcome the poorer physical conditions.

4. The extreme heat and cold of some environments means that they are not used for agriculture because the large amount of money needed to adapt them would not allow a profit to be made.

### (b) Controls on the Efficiency of Production

The physical environment also determines whether the processes needed to produce the crops or animals can operate efficiently (e.g. planting and harvesting of some crops by machines is impossible on steep slopes).

### (c) Change and Physical Controls

1. Farmers and governments may decide to try to overcome the limitations of the physical environment.

2. This involves an increase of inputs into the farm, making the system more intensive. The processes and inputs of the system often change as a result of the increased inputs.

**Table 11.2** Some methods of overcoming the physical limitations to farming

| Method |
| --- |
| 1. Irrigation to improve water supply |
| 2. New seed varieties to increase the yield |
| 3. Fertilisers to improve the soil |
| 4. Pesticides to reduce pest damage |
| 5. Ditches to improve drainage |
| 6. Greenhouses to lengthen the growing season and reduce the risk of frost damage |
| 7. Hedge planting to reduce wind damage |
| 8. Terracing to reduce slope angles |

# 11.4 Social and political controls

## (a) Social Controls

**Table 11.3** Social controls

| Control | Nature of the control |
| --- | --- |
| Land tenure | Improvements to the farm are more likely when the farmer owns the land, as farmers who rent the land may be evicted without proper compensation for any improvements they have made. |
| Social customs | Some societies prohibit the production of certain animals and crops. |
| Laws of inheritance | Can lead to farms becoming fragmented and small. Land is wasted by increased field boundaries and time is wasted moving between fragmented plots. The income available for improvements from a smaller farm is less. |
| Population pressure | Can cause the existing and newly cleared land to be farmed too intensively without proper consideration of the balance of the ecosystem (see Section 4.5(b)). The result is lower yields and soil erosion. |
| Education levels | A low level of education usually means that farmers are less willing to introduce new techniques, are less likely to understand the controls on them and the effects of any change that they introduce. |

## (b) Political Controls

1. Governments act either independently or together with other governments (e.g. within the EEC) to carry out a number of policies.

2. The aims of these policies vary, depending on the nature of agriculture in a particular country or group of countries, but fall into two broad categories:

   (a) to support the farming practices that are currently operating
   (b) to stimulate change in the agricultural system.

3. The farmer may be forced by law to adopt a government scheme or be influenced by the benefits of the scheme to consider it as a factor in the decision-making process.

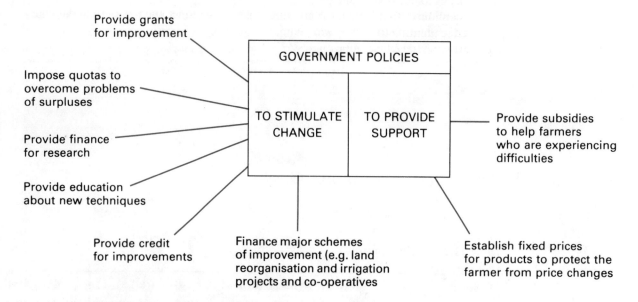

**Figure 11.3**  Some ways in which governments can influence farmers' decisions

## 11.5  Economic controls

### (a) The Decision-making Equation

1. If farmers are trying to make a profit by selling their produce they must estimate the costs which they will incur and subtract these from the money that they will get from the sale of the produce, which will depend on the yield and the sale price.

> Profit = (Yield × Sale price) + Other income (e.g. grants) − Costs

**Figure 11.4**  The farmer's decision-making equation

2. The farmer must do this for each section of land on the farm for each of the crops and animals the physical environment allows.
3. A farmer will usually produce more than one commodity to reduce the risk of crop failure and a fall in the sale price, to maintain the fertility of the soil and to ensure that the land is used intensively by planting and harvesting different crops in different seasons.

**(b) Sale Price and Costs**

1. The farmer is trying to get a price for the products of the farm that will cover the cost of production and transport and at the·same time make a profit.
2. The sale price of the product is affected by:

   (a) the levels of supply and demand. The sale price reflects the balance between supply and demand; if the supply exceeds the demand then the price may fall as there is a surplus; if demand is greater than the supply the sale price may rise.
   (b) the cost of the inputs. If the costs are too high and push up the sale price too much the demand for the product may fall and the farmer may not make a profit.

3. Even when the farmer's decision is simplified by the fixing of the sale price of a product by the government the farmer still has to take into account the costs of the inputs.
4. Crops and animals that are produced in areas where their optimum growing conditions are not found will need a higher level of inputs to gain a particular yield and will therefore cost more to produce.

**(c) Accessibility, Cost and Variations in Land Use**

1. The cost of producing a particular crop on different sections of the farm and different areas around the market varies. Less accessible fields and areas have higher costs due to the increased transport costs.
2. Increased cost with reduced accessibility means that the farmer has to consider the profit that can be gained from a piece of land if different crops are grown on it.
3. As accessibility decreases so does the value of the land. Because the more valuable land needs to be farmed more intensively to pay for it and because accessibility is partly related to distance a general land use pattern emerges where the intensity of the land use decreases with distance from the farm buildings and the market.
4. Products which can be farmed intensively and make a high profit (e.g. market gardening) are found near the market; those that are not (e.g. sheep farming) are found further away.

## 11.6 Differences in agriculture between developed and developing countries

**(a) The Nature of the Differences**

1. In the developing countries the controls on the decision-making process limit the choices available to the farmer to a greater extent than in developed countries (see Section 9.3).
2. The agricultural systems that have resulted from this have different characteristics.

**Table 11.4** Summary of the major differences

| Least developed countries | | Most developed countries |
|---|---|---|
| Low | Amount of technology | High |
| Low | Level of technology | High |
| Low | Amount of government support | High |
| High | Percentage of total workforce employed in agriculture | Low |
| High | Percentage of agricultural workers involved in subsistence farming | Low |
| Low | Productivity per worker | High |
| Low | Average profit per hectare | High |
| Low | Average investment per hectare | High |
| Low | Average farm size | High |
| High | Percentage of farms that are fragmented | Low |
| Poor | Access to the market by efficient transport | Good |
| Low | Level of education among farmers | High |

3. The differences represent a large gap in the level of agricultural development between the developing and developed countries.

### (b) Lessening the Gap

1. Any improvements to the agricultural systems of the developing countries must take into account the level of development of a particular country and the particular controls under which farming operates.
2. Attempts to increase food production by intensifying agriculture is sometimes referred to as the 'green revolution'.
3. Intensification involves the introduction of high-yield seed varieties, money for projects (e.g. irrigation), cheaper loans to farmers, intermediate technology, the development of better access to the market.
4. Improvements are usually funded by a combination of national governments and world aid organisations (see Section 9.4 (d)).

## 11.7 The effect of agriculture on the natural environment

### (a) Agriculture and Ecosystems

1. Farms occupy and change natural ecosystems to the extent that few natural ecosystems still exist.
2. The main change involves the clearance of the natural vegetation to allow the growth of crops for human and animal consumption.
3. The effect that this has had on ecosystems varies depending on the nature of the ecosystem and the type of agricultural practices.
4. Ecosystems can be damaged to the extent that they are no longer of use to agriculture (see Section 4.5 (b) and Table 6.3).
5. Because different types of ecosystem are linked agriculture in one ecosystem can affect the components of another.

**Table 11.5** Some of the effects of agriculture on ecosystems

| Agricultural activity | Effect on ecosystem |
|---|---|
| Clearance of vegetation | Landscapes altered; habitats of plants and animals destroyed to the extent that species become extinct. Soil erosion more likely. |
| Pesticides | Enter food chains causing the death of insects, birds and fish and the pollution of water supplies. |
| Fertilisers | Become dissolved in both river and groundwater causing high nitrate levels in drinking water (thought to be responsible for some illnesses in humans) and the growth of algae and weeds in rivers. |
| Irrigation | Increases the salt content of the soil making it of little use for agriculture. |
| Overgrazing | Removes the vegetation cover to the extent that the soil becomes exposed and is eroded. |

1. Conservation aims to preserve the natural ecosystem as far as is possible.
2. The aims of conservation are often in conflict with the need to make the highest profit or grow the maximum amount of food.
3. This conflict often leads to a compromise solution.
4. Where areas of countryside are recognised as being unique they can be preserved by law or by agreement (e.g. Sites of Special Scientific Interest).

# 11.8 Agriculture examples

**Table 11.6** Agriculture examples

| Named examples of | Factual information needed | Your named example |
|---|---|---|
| 1. Farming systems (arable, pastoral, mixed, intensive, extensive, commercial, subsistence) | Location of system, description of system. Nature of controls that influence decision-making. | 1.(a)<br>1.(b)<br>1.(c) |
| 2. Farm where decision has been influenced by government | Location and name of farm. Details of how government policy has influenced farmer's decisions. | 2. |
| 3. Farm or area where accessibility has influenced land use | Location and name of area or farm. Details of effect of accessibility on land use (sketch map). | 3. |

| | | |
|---|---|---|
| 4. Examples of farm or area where improvements have been attempted by using modern technology | Location and name of area or farm. Details of improvement. Effect on production. | 4. |
| 5. Examples of farm or area where improvements have been attempted by using intermediate technology | Location and name of area or farm. Details of improvement. Effect on production. | 5. |
| 6. Farm or area where agricultural processes have caused environmental problems | Location and name of farm or area. Details of processes that have caused environmental problems. Solutions to the problems. | 6. |
| 7. Farm or area where conservation techniques are in use | Location and name of farm or area. Details of how techniques operate and their effects on farm production. | 7. |

## 11.9   Questions and answers

### (a)  Multiple-choice and Completion Questions

**1** Which of the crops and animals is most likely to be produced in the area shown by the climate graph below?

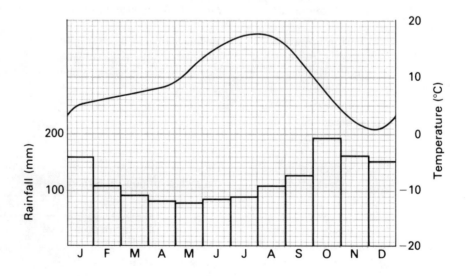

Climate graph

A wheat
B sheep
C citrus fruit
D rice
E rubber

2 Which of the statements below is a characteristic of agriculture in developing countries?

A Productivity per worker is high.
B The percentage of the working population employed in agriculture is high.
C The average investment per hectare is high.
D The profit per hectare is high.
E The amount of government support is high.

3 Which of the statements below is least likely to be the result of population pressure?

A New land is cleared for cultivation.
B People leave the rural areas to try to find work in urban areas.
C Soil erosion begins due to overgrazing.
D Existing agricultural land is farmed more extensively.
E The use of fertilisers increases.

4 Complete the table below by adding possible solutions to the problems of the physical environment that are listed:

Physical environment problems and their solutions

| Problem | Solution |
|---|---|
| 1. Too little water<br>2. Infertile soil<br>3. Crop damage by pests<br>4. Waterlogged soils<br>5. Steep slopes | Fertilisers to improve the soil<br>Pesticides to reduce pest damage |

5 For this question one or more of the responses given are correct. Decide which of the responses is (are) correct. Then choose:

A if 1, 2 and 3 are all correct
B if 1 and 2 only are correct
C if 2 and 3 only are correct
D if 1 only is correct
E if 3 only is correct.

Which of the events listed below may happen when a government introduces milk quotas?

1. The farmer produces less milk.
2. The farmer changes the land use on the farm.
3. The surplus of milk is reduced.

167

**Example 11.1**

(a)   Look at the diagram and the passage about a farm in South-East Asia.

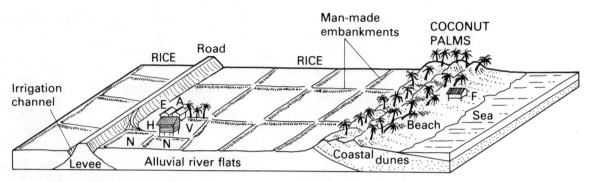

A – animal shelters: buffalo, chickens, ducks
E – equipment shed
F – fishing shed: equipment, boat

H – house on stilts
N – rice seedling nursery plots
V – vegetable garden

The farm covers an area of 7 hectares. The main cash crop is rice, but the farmer also sells coconuts, poultry and fish. The vegetables are mainly grown to feed the family.

The rice fields are flooded when the monsoon arrives, but more water is added from the canals if it is needed. The farmer irrigates the vegetables too.

He buys fertiliser, seed and poultry food from a nearby town. His other expenses are rates, water, electricity and the workers needed to harvest the rice.
His farm is profitable and he is saving to buy a tractor.

A farm in South-East Asia:

(i)  Is the farm a large or small one?
(ii) List four of the farm's inputs.

(b)   (i)   Suggest why the farmer keeps a buffalo.
(ii)  Suggest why the farmhouse is built on stilts.
(iii) Rice cannot be grown in the coastal dune area. Suggest why.
(iv)  Suggest why a group of palm trees was planted near the farmhouse.

(c) Using the figures in the table below complete the rainfall and temperature graphs opposite:

| Month | Temperature (°C) | Rainfall (mm) |
|---|---|---|
| September | 27 | 200 |
| October | 27 | 300 |
| November | 26 | 660 |
| December | 25 | 630 |

(d)   (i)   State the lowest monthly temperature.
(ii)  Is the total yearly rainfall best described as low, moderate or heavy?
(iii) Suggest two reasons why the farmer is able to grow several crops of vegetables each year.
(iv)  Name the months when the farmer goes fishing.
(v)   Suggest one reason why the farmer chooses to go fishing in these months.

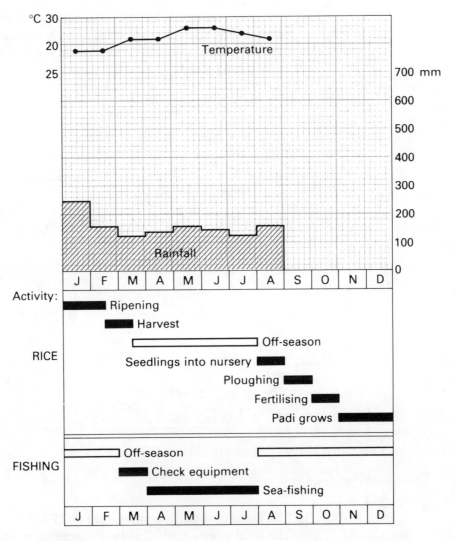

Climate of the area, and the farmer's activities throughout the year

(e) 'Economic activity may be seen as a system with inputs, processes and outputs.'
   (i) For a named factory or industrial works that you have studied, describe its main inputs, processes and outputs.
   (ii) Explain the advantages of its location.

(**LEAG** syllabus B question 4 1988)

**Solution 11.1**

(a) (i) The farm is a large one.
   (ii) Four inputs are:
      1. fertiliser
      2. seed
      3. poultry food
      4. labour

(b) (i) The farmer may keep a buffalo to plough the fields.
   (ii) The farmhouse may be built on stilts to stop it from being flooded when the rice fields are flooded.

(iii) The rice crop needs to be flooded; the sand of the coastal dunes would allow the water to drain away too quickly.

(iv) The palm trees may have been planted to protect the farmhouse from strong winds.

(c) See the figure below:

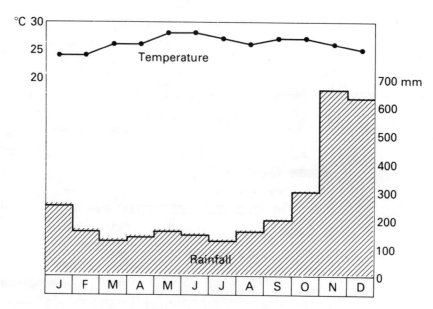

Completed climate graph of the area

(d) (i) The lowest monthly temperature is 25°C.

(ii) The total yearly rainfall is best described as heavy.

(iii) The farmer is able to grow several crops of vegetables because:

**Reason 1**
The climate of the area is hot and wet all year.
**Reason 2**
The farmer has money to buy fertiliser so the soil will not become infertile.

(iv) The farmer goes fishing in April, May, June and July.

(v) The farmer may choose to go fishing in these months because it is the off-season for rice growing, so rather than waste the time the farmer fishes to make more profit.

(e) (i) **Named factory or industrial works: Craft Design**
The main inputs into the factory are small amounts of hardwood, skilled machine operators and unskilled packers, wood lathes and electricity to power them and small vans to distribute the finished product. Some of the profit from the sale of the goods is used to update the machines and pay the production costs. The main processes in the factory are to turn the wood on the lathes to produce small trinkets. The trinkets are then sanded, polished and packaged by hand. The main outputs are a variety of small wooden articles (e.g. mice, bowls, pen holders).

(ii) The factory is in the town of Carterton. The advantages of this location are firstly it is near to the Cotswolds whose tourists provide a large market; this reduces the distribution costs. Secondly, it is the home town of the managing director who, because of his local contacts, could secure a loan to set up the factory and sell his products to the local tourist shops. Thirdly, the factory is in a modern unit provided by the council at a cheaper than usual rate. This provides a healthy working environment and lowers production costs. Finally, the local schools are a source of labour to be trained as machine operators at a low cost under the Youth Training Scheme.

**Example 11.2**

(a)  Look at the information below:

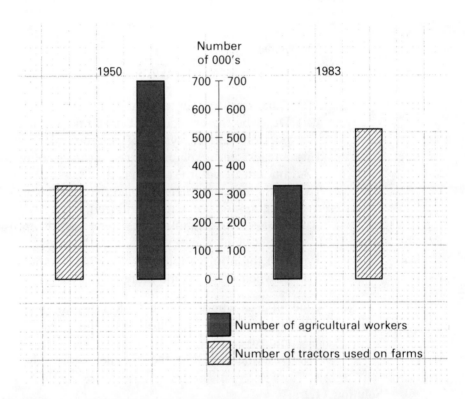

The number of agricultural workers and tractors in agriculture in the UK

(i) How many more tractors were there in 1983 than in 1950?
(ii) Describe the change in the number of agricultural workers between 1950 and 1983.
(iii) Give one reason for this change.
(iv) Name two farming processes that can be helped by tractors.

(b) Look at the diagram below:

| | 1950 | | | | 1986 | | |
|---|---|---|---|---|---|---|---|
| | Areas under cultivation | Amount produced | Yield (tonnes per hectare) | | Areas under cultivation | Amount produced | Yield (tonnes per hectare) |
| Wheat | ▪ ▪ ▪ ▪ ▪▪ ▪▪ ▪▪ | ▪ ▪ ▪ ▪ | 2.6 | | ▪▪ ▪▪▪ ▪▪▪ ▪▪▪ ▪▪▪ ▪▪▪ ▪▪▪ | ▪▪▪▪ ▪▪▪▪ ▪▪▪▪ ▪▪▪▪ ▪▪▪▪ ▪▪▪▪ | 6.9 |
| Potatoes | ▪ ▪ ▪ ▪ ▪ | ▪▪ ▪▪ ▪▪▪ ▪▪▪ ▪▪▪ ▪▪▪ | 19.3 | | ▪ ▪ | ▪ ▪▪ ▪▪ ▪▪ ▪▪ ▪▪ | 32.2 |

▪ = 500 000 tonnes      ▪ = 100 000 hectares

Approximate figures for wheat and potato production in the UK

(i) What does the term 'yield' mean?
(ii) Describe the changes that have taken place in the area used for potatoes and the 'yield' of potatoes between 1950 and 1986.
(iii) Suggest and explain one reason to account for the drop in the amount of potatoes produced.
(iv) Using only the diagram give two reasons for the increase in the total amount of wheat produced.
(v) Suggest three methods that may have been used to increase the wheat yield.
(vi) Use the information in the diagram to show that the production of wheat has become more intensive.

(c) Name an area where agriculture has become more intensive.
(i) Describe how agriculture in the area has been made more intensive.
(ii) Describe the effect that this has had on the environment.

**Solution 11.2**

(a)   (i) There were 200 000 more tractors in 1983 than in 1950.
(ii) The number of agricultural workers has decreased between 1950 and 1983 from 700 000 to 330 000.
(iii) There are fewer agricultural workers because more tractors are used, reducing the need for agricultural workers.
(iv) Ploughing and sowing.

(b)   (i) The term 'yield' is used to describe the amount of produce from an area of land, usually measured in hectares.
(ii) The area used to grow potatoes has decreased by 300 000 hectares from 500 000 hectares in 1950 to 200 000 hectares in 1986. The yield has increased by 17 tonnes per hectare from 19 tonnes per hectare in 1950 to 36 tonnes per hectare in 1986.

(iii) The total amount of potatoes could have fallen due to a fall in demand as a result of competition from foods such as pasta and rice.

(iv) **Reason 1**
The amount of wheat produced has increased because the yield per hectare has increased.
**Reason 2**
The amount of wheat produced has increased because the area of farmland used to grow wheat has increased.

(v) **Method 1**
The development and introduction of new varieties of seeds that have a higher yield.
**Method 2**
The increased use of fertilisers.
**Method 3**
The increased use of pesticides.

(vi) The production of wheat has become more intensive because the amount that has been produced has increased by over 5 times, but the area under cultivation has only doubled. In order to achieve this the amount of investment has had to increase so that the yield per hectare has increased from 2.6 tonnes per hectare in 1950 to 6.9 tonnes per hectare in 1986.

(c) **Named area – the Norfolk Broads**

(i) The Norfolk Broads is an area of marshland and navigable waterways. Some of the marshland has been reclaimed for use as pastureland. The removal of reeds, the application of increased amounts of fertiliser, and the installation of more efficient pumps are the methods that have been introduced to intensify production, by increasing the quality of the pasture, thus allowing more animals to graze.

(ii) The improved drainage has caused the water table to drop and the land to sink below the level of the waterways. The fertiliser has entered the waterways increasing pollution. This together with the removal of the reeds has reduced the numbers of fish, birds and insects as their habitats have been removed.

(c) **Answers to Multiple-choice and Completion Questions**

**1 B**
**2 B**
**3 D**
**4** See the table below:

Physical environment problems and their solutions

| Problem | Solution |
|---|---|
| 1. Too little water | Irrigation to improve water supply. |
| 2. Infertile soil | Fertilisers to improve the soil |
| 3. Crop damage by pests | Pesticides to reduce pest damage |
| 4. Waterlogged soils | Ditches to improve drainage |
| 5. Steep slopes | Terracing to reduce slope angles. |

**5 A**

173

# 12 Secondary Industry

## 12.1 The characteristics of secondary industry

### (a) Secondary Industry as a System

1. Secondary or manufacturing industry is concerned with changing raw materials from the primary sector or assembling parts, to form a semi-finished or finished product.
2. The product from a secondary industry can be used as the raw material of another secondary industry, or it can be a finished product.
3. Secondary industry as a whole or as an individual factory can be viewed as a system with inputs which are processed as they flow through the system becoming the outputs from the system.

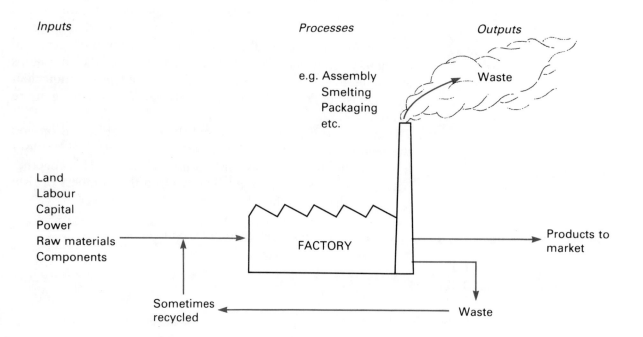

**Figure 12.1**  The secondary industry as a system

### (b) The Organisation of Secondary Industry

1. Secondary industry can be divided broadly into traditional and modern.
2. Traditional or craft industry, characterised by the absence of modern technology, is often organised on a family basis and operates from the home of the family or a small workshop. It employs most of the secondary sector's workforce in the developing countries.

174

3. Modern industry, characterised by its use of modern technology, is organised into firms or companies which operate from plants, factories or workshops.
4. Modern industry varies enormously in size and complexity from the small-scale, family-run business which operates from a single small plant or factory, produces a single product in one country and employs a small number of people, to a **multinational company** which operates in many different countries, has many factories, employs a large number of peopie and produces many different products.
5. Large companies have often formed by taking over or merging with other companies which produce the same product (**horizontal integration**) or by taking over their suppliers or distributors (**vertical integration**).

## 12.2 Industrial change and the decision-making process

### (a) The Need for Decision Making

1. An individual firm operates in a system where the benefits of the factory location, the costs of its inputs, the demand for and price of its products, the competition from new and existing firms and the available technology are constantly changing.
2. Firms need to make decisions about their response to these changes.
3. The decision that is taken decides whether the firm will grow, decline or stagnate and may lead to the creation of new firms and the choice of new locations.
4. The decision of one firm may affect linked firms.

### (b) Alternative Strategies

1. The decision may be made by either an individual or a group of managers or in communist countries by the government.
2. The decision makers are faced with a number of alternative strategies:

    (a) expand or reduce production at an existing factory
    (b) close an existing factory
    (c) open a new factory
    (d) close an existing factory and open a new factory
    (e) join together a number of factories at an existing or a new site
    (f) produce a different product
    (g) develop a new market.

### (c) Choosing a Strategy

1. The choice of strategy depends on how the decision makers perceive the factors that are influencing them. Two different decision makers may choose different strategies even if the factors influencing them are the same.
2. The decision makers must consider the alternative strategies, given the resources available to them, so that the most profitable decision is reached i.e. where the income minus the costs is greatest.

3. Production costs are reduced if **economies of scale** (the savings in production costs as a result of the increased size of factory) can be achieved. The savings that result have to be balanced against the increased distribution costs to the market.
4. Where the decisions are influenced by a government the choice of strategy and location is partly based on profit but also on the political and social benefits of one strategy rather than another.
5. Where the decision results in factory closure the result can be the industrial decline of a region (see Section 9.7).
6. Where a new factory is a possible strategy the decision makers must look at the locational factors of a number of potentially favourable sites to decide which is most suitable for their industry.

**Table 12.1** Locational factors for secondary industry

| Locational factor | Questions that the decision makers need to answer for each potential site |
|---|---|
| Access to raw materials | How much will it cost to collect the amount we need? Is the cheapest form of transport available? |
| Access to market | How much will it cost to get our products to the market? Is the cheapest form of transport available? |
| Power source | Is a suitable power source available at a reasonable price? |
| Labour force | Is the required number of workers with the necessary skills available? If not has the environment of the area sufficient quality to attract them? Are the wage rates relatively low? |
| Agglomeration | Are there any industries in the area that we can benefit from? |
| Capital supply | Is capital available for development in the area? Do we have personal contacts with people who will lend money? Can we save money by converting an old industrial building? |
| Government influence | Are there any grants offered for new industry in the area to reduce building, re-training, rates and taxation costs? How easy is it to get an industrial development certificate? |
| Site requirements | Is there a cheap site in the area which is the correct size, flat, well drained, stable and which has planning permission and no opposition from the local community? Can a site be altered to meet our needs? How much will the alterations cost? |
| Environmental quality | Does the area offer the workforce a range of leisure pursuits and an attractive landscape? |

7. Sometimes, the benefits to be gained from moving to a new more profitable location do not outweigh the costs of moving, so the original factory will remain even though it is no longer in the best location. When this happens **industrial inertia** is operating.

# 12.3 Locational factors and the distribution of industry

## (a) The General Distribution of Industry

1. The distribution of industry is a result of the locational decisions that have been taken in the past. The older a factory is the greater the likelihood that it is no longer in the best location.
2. Modern industry tends to be concentrated rather than dispersed because some areas within a country and the world have a more favourable set of location factors than others.
3. This pattern is more pronounced in the developing countries where most modern industry is located in coastal cities because they offer the best set of locational advantages.

**Table 12.2** Advantages of coastal cities in developing countries for modern industry

| Factor | Advantage |
| --- | --- |
| Labour | A higher level of skill than the rest of the country and still non-unionised and cheap. |
| Power | Coastal cities often have a power network so there is no need to generate power for a new factory. Electricity is cheaper because imported fuel does not have to be transported inland and because the power stations are often larger to meet the demands of the city. |
| Market | The coastal city is often the main market in the country. Inland transport links often run from the coastal city to the rest of the home market. Access to the world market is possible through the port which is often part of the coastal city. |
| Raw materials | Raw materials can be imported through the port or brought to the coast from inland by the road and rail links. |

4. Some areas have a set of locational advantages that attract a particular industry (e.g. textiles) which dominates the industrial structure of the region.

## (b) The Distribution of Industry in Urban Areas

See Section 8.3 (d).

## (c) Locational Factors and the Distribution of Different Types of Industry

1. The location of some industries is mainly controlled by one of the locational factors.
2. **Footloose** industries have a large choice of locations because they use light raw materials to produce a light product. Their main locational requirement is therefore access to an efficient transport network for distribution to the market which can be found on the edge of most towns and near the rail or motorway network.
3. **High technology** industries have developed in recent decades and use or produce advanced technology. They benefit from agglomeration and are located in areas of high environmental quality that can attract the necessary highly skilled workforce.

177

**Table 12.3** Types of industry dominated by one locational factor

| Dominant factor | Industry type | Reasons |
|---|---|---|
| Raw material | Raw material orientated, e.g. steel industry, coal-fired power stations | Industries that use large quantities of heavy, bulky raw materials which lose weight during processing are typical raw material orientated or **heavy** industries. They are found at the site where it is cheapest to transport the necessary raw materials. This is usually at the site of the extraction of the raw material that is most expensive to transport, or its entry point into the country (if the raw materials are imported). |
| Market | Market orientated e.g. baking | Industries that add weight or bulk during processing or are producing perishable products are typical market orientated industries because the cost of transporting the product to the market is higher than the cost of collecting the raw materials together. When the market is spread throughout a country they are usually found scattered through a country in towns and cities. |
| Power | Power orientated e.g. aluminium smelting | Modern industry needs a power source. Where power is needed in large quantities or in a special form then the factory will be found at its power source to reduce transport and production costs. |
| Labour | Labour orientated e.g. electrical engineering | An industry that needs a labour force with special skills or a large cheap labour force will be labour orientated. |

## 12.4 Industrial pollution

See Table 6.3.

## 12.5 Secondary industry examples

**Table 12.4** Secondary industry examples

| Named examples of | Factual information needed | Your named example |
|---|---|---|
| 1. An industrial system | Name and location of industry. Description of inputs, outputs and processes. | 1. |
| 2. A multinational company | Name of company. Description of products, location of some of factories and organisation of the company. | 2. |
| 3. An industry that has changed to continue to make a profit | Name and location of industry. Description of the reasons for change and the changes that have taken place. | 3. |
| 4. An industrial concentration | Name and location of area of concentration. Description of the industries found in the area and the advantages of the area for them. | 4. |
| 5. Raw material orientated industry | Name and location of industry. Advantages of location. | 5. |
| 6. Market orientated industry | | 6. |
| 7. Labour orientated industry | | 7. |
| 8. Power orientated industry | | 8. |
| 9. Footloose industry | | 9. |
| 10. Urban area | Name and location of area. Description and location of industry within the area. Reasons for location. | 10. |
| 11. Industrial pollution | Name and location of industry causing pollution. Type of pollution, its effects and attempts at control. | 11. |

# 12.6 Questions and answers

### (a) Multiple-choice and Completion Questions

1 Which of the people listed below works in secondary (manufacturing) industry?

   **A** a truck driver
   **B** a ticket collector
   **C** a coal miner
   **D** a shoemaker
   **E** a solicitor

2 Which of the industries listed below would be most likely to be located on a modern industrial estate?

   **A** an oil refinery
   **B** a coal-fired power station
   **C** a factory making computers
   **D** a chemical works
   **E** a vegetable canning plant

3 Which of the industries listed below is most likely to cause acid rain?

   **A** a hydro-electric power station
   **B** a car assembly plant
   **C** a bakery
   **D** a coal-fired power station
   **E** a sawmill

4 Complete the diagram opposite by putting the correct word, from the list below, in the correct box.

   Waste
   Inputs
   Power
   Outputs
   Packing

5 For this question one or more of the responses given are correct. Decide which of the responses is (are) correct. Then choose:

   **A** if 1, 2 and 3 are all correct
   **B** if 1 and 2 only are correct
   **C** if 2 and 3 only are correct
   **D** if 1 only is correct
   **E** if 3 only is correct.

A footloose industry:

1. has a wide choice of locations
2. needs good access to efficient transport
3. uses light raw materials.

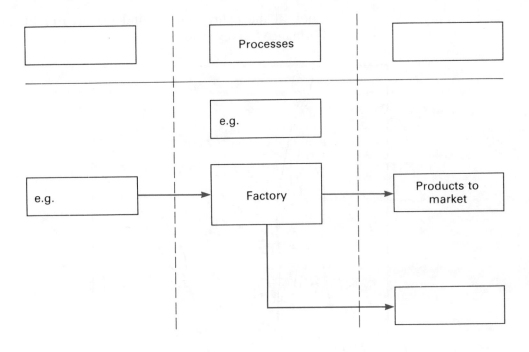

Simplified diagram of a secondary industrial system

**(b) Structured Questions**

**Example 12.1**

Look at the 1:50000 Ordnance Survey map extract at the back of the book.

(a)   (i) Measure the road distance from the works at grid reference 678980 to the nearest motorway junction.

(ii) What do the symbols at the following grid references represent:

1.685990
2.672968
3.637995

(b)   (i) Describe the site of the works at grid reference 667962.

(ii) Describe the situation of the works at grid reference 643999.

(iii) Find the industrial estates in grid squares 6296 and 6797. State two similarities in their situation.

(iv) Explain the advantages of the locations of these industrial estates.

(v) Describe the types of industry that might choose to locate on them.

(c) Look at the figure below. Find the area of the sketch map on the Ordnance Survey map.

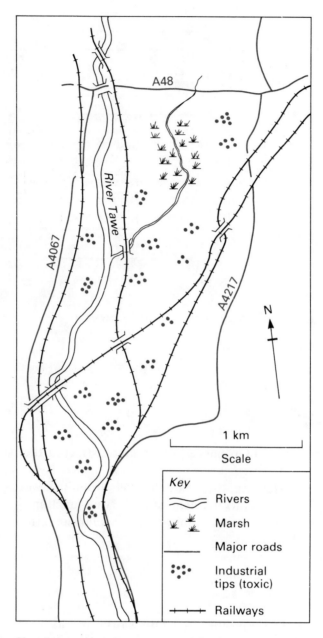

Sketch map showing an area of Swansea as it was in 1967

(i) The Ordnance Survey map is more recent than the sketch map. Describe the main changes that have taken place in the area of the sketch map bounded by the three A roads (A48, A4217 and A4067).

(ii) Suggest why the changes have been made.

**Solution 12.1**

(a)  (i) 2.2 kilometres.
    (ii) 1. Electricity transmission line.
        2. Spoil heap, refuse tip or dump.
        3. Freight line, siding or tramway.

(b)  (i)  The works are sited on the eastern bank of the River Tawe on flat or very gently sloping land.

(ii)  The works are situated next to a freight line and 1 kilometre from a motorway; both of these transport links run in an east-to-west direction. The centre of Swansea lies approximately 6 kilometres to the south and can be reached by following the B4489.

(iii)  **Similarity 1**
Both industrial estates are on the edge of the built-up area of Swansea.
**Similarity 2**
Both estates are within 4 kilometres of a motorway junction.

(iv)  Both industrial estates have the advantage of being close to the motorway for the collection of their raw materials and the distribution of their products. In addition, Swansea is a potential market and source of raw materials and labour. Both estates have open space around them which could be used for expansion and provides a better working environment. This last point together with the attractions of the coastline to the south and the other leisure amenities (e.g. the golf course at grid reference 663990, the marina at 657925) may provide the type of environment that enables firms to gather the best possible workforce.

(v)  Industries that use roads to transport their relatively light raw materials and products and that need a pleasant working and leisure environment to attract a skilled workforce will locate on the estate. The type of industries that therefore might use the estates includes wholesale and storage warehouses, light industry and commercial offices.

(c)  (i)  A number of features have disappeared and appeared in the area. The only remaining freight line, siding or tramway runs down the eastern edge of the area; only one of the spoil heaps, refuse tips or dumps remains at grid reference 672968. The area of marsh to the north of the area has been drained, and a lake created, which is ringed by a new road, along which an industrial estate has begun to be built. A number of paths have been created or extended mainly in grid square 6795. Some mixed woodland has been planted between the A4217 and the remaining freight line, siding or tramway and in grid square 6695.

(ii)  The area as it was in 1967 showed the signs of industrial pollution. The toxic waste tips were probably a danger to the local population who played or walked across the area. The area is a valuable section of land, located as it is close to the built-up area of Swansea. Without the removal of the tips and unwanted railway lines and the tree-planting the area would not be attractive as a site for new industries and leisure activities and would therefore be wasted. The creation of the new road is probably designed to provide access to the area for new industries.

## Example 12.2

(a) Study the photographs below:

Some examples of small-scale craft industries found in developing countries

(i) With the help of the photographs explain what you understand by the term 'small-scale craft industries'.

(ii) Why are these industries important to countries in the developing world?

(b) (i) Study the figure below:

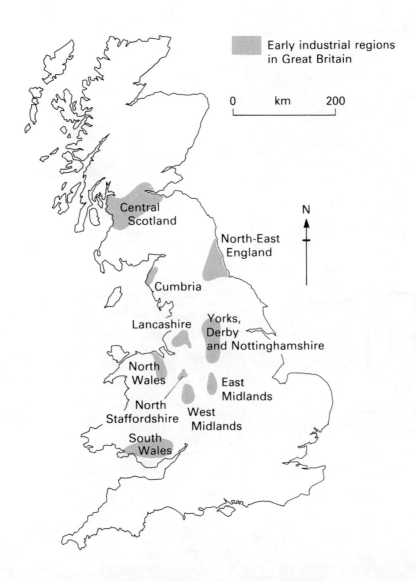

The location of early industrial regions in Great Britain

Account for the concentration of industry in the regions shown.

(ii) Why is modern industrial growth in developed countries such as Great Britain now more widespread?

(c) One type of modern industrial development is a science park: a centre for high-technology industries. Using the information given in the figure below answer the questions that follow:

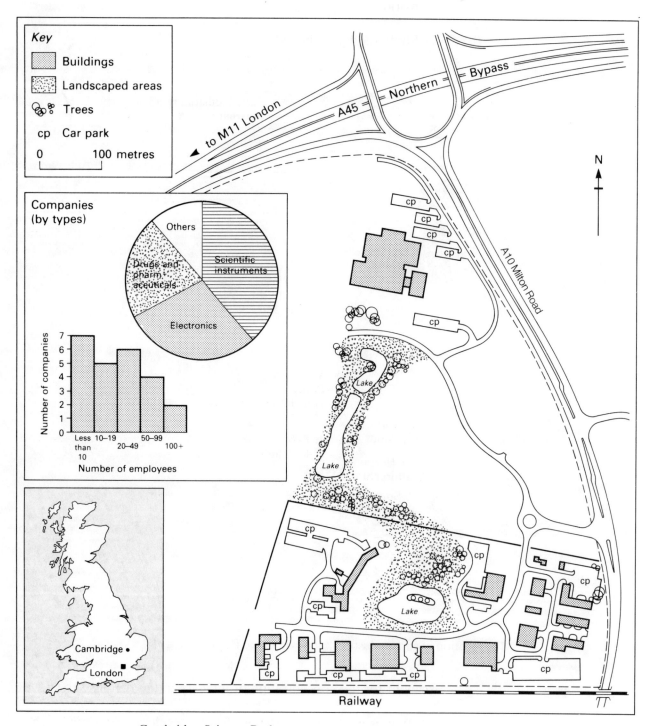

Cambridge Science Park

(i) Describe and comment on the main details of the industries, the location and the layout of the Cambridge Science Park.
(ii) What effects may the growth of the science park have on the surrounding area?
(iii) What are the advantages of locating a science park in a university town such as Cambridge?

(**MEG** syllabus B paper 2 question E9 1988)

**Solution 12.2**

(a)   (i)  Small-scale craft industries are characterised by the absence of modern technology (pictures 1, 6 and 7), they are often organised on a family basis and operate from the home of the family or a small workshop (pictures 1 and 7), they are labour intensive (pictures 2, 5 and 6) and produce unique products that require skilled labour (pictures 2, 3 and 5).

     (ii)  They are important to countries in the developing world because firstly, they account for most of the employment in the secondary sector. Secondly, they use technology that is appropriate to the level of development and thirdly, they can be easily located in rural areas to provide an alternative form of employment to agriculture.

(b)   (i)  The early industrial regions shown in the figure are located on the coalfields that were the first to be developed. At the time, coal provided the main source of power to drive the machinery used within the regions. As coal is a heavy and bulky commodity it is expensive to transport; also, at the time, transport networks were less efficient and widespread so most modern industries had to locate on the coalfields to reduce their costs.

     (ii)  Industrial growth is now more widespread because the locational factors are now available in a greater number of places. The creation of national grids has enabled industries using electricity to locate almost anywhere within a country. The increase in the variety of transport modes, and the area that is served by transport networks, has reduced the need for industries to be located close to their market and/or source of raw materials. Skilled industrial labour has become more widespread and has increased in mobility.

As the locational factors for an industry have changed (e.g. a new source of a raw material) new firms have chosen new locations, while others have remained in the same location, thus increasing the spread of industry.

New locational factors, such as the quality of the environment, have become important causing new areas to become industrialised.

(c)   (i)  Approximately 89% of the companies on the park are involved in the production of drugs and pharmaceuticals or electronics or scientific instruments. Only 6 out of the 24 companies on the park employ more than 50 people; 7 companies employ fewer than 10. The type of product and the generally small workforce suggest that the companies use a high level of technological equipment and employ a highly skilled workforce.

The park is located in Cambridge to the north of London on a site that is removed from other buildings. The site lies to the west of the A10 and to the south of the A45; a railway line forms its southern boundary. The site entrance is within 1 kilometre of the Northern Bypass which provides good access to London via the M11 and to the rest of Cambridge.

The site is laid out along three 'main' roads from which a series of feeder roads form cul-de-sacs. The cul-de-sacs in the northern and southern sections of the site provide access to a number of well-spaced industrial buildings and car parks; the central section of the park appears only partially developed as there are no buildings. Part of the site has been landscaped with lakes and trees.

(ii) The park may have had a visual impact on the surrounding area as most of the landscaping has taken place in the centre of the site rather than on the edge. The employees of the companies may have moved to the area creating additional demand for housing.

(iii) The research projects that form a part of the work of universities may provide a market for the companies on a nearby science park. The researchers and graduates of the university may be a source of the specialist skilled labour that is needed by the companies on the park.

### (b) Answers to Multiple-choice and Completion Questions

**1 D**
**2 C**
**3 D**
**4** See the figure below:

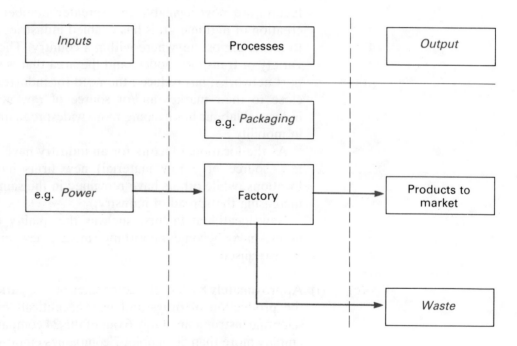

Simplified diagram of a secondary industrial system

**5 A**

# 13 Tertiary Industry

## 13.1 The characteristics of tertiary industry

### (a) Tertiary Industry

1. **Tertiary industry** is concerned with providing a service and is sometimes known as the **service industry**.
2. Tertiary industry includes a wide range of different services. It is sometimes split, by calling some services (e.g. research) **quaternary industry**.

### (b) Types of Tertiary Industry

1. The tertiary industries can be divided into a number of different groups.

**Table 13.1**   Different types of services

| Type | Examples |
|------|----------|
| 1. Public administration | Civil service, town hall |
| 2. Supply of public services | Waste disposal, water, health |
| 3. Transport | Road, rail, air, sea |
| 4. Personal | Accountants, barristers, hairdressers |
| 5. Commerce | Insurance, banking, building societies, offices |
| 6. Leisure | Hotels, theatre, television, radio, sports centre |
| 7. Distribution | Warehouses, wholesale and retail selling |
| 8. Defence | Army, navy, air force |

2. Some services are used by industry (e.g. freight trains) and some by the population as a whole (e.g theatres) but most are used by both (e.g. barristers).
3. Public services are administered and paid for by government funds collected from the population as a whole (e.g. defence and household waste disposal). Private services are administered by companies and paid for by the people and companies that use them.

### (c) Hierarchies of Services

1. A hierarchy of services can be recognised.
2. High-order services at the top of the hierarchy have a larger sphere of influence, a greater range and a larger threshold population than services lower down the hierarchy (see Fig. 8.1).

## 13.2 The growth of tertiary industry

### (a) The Amount of Growth

1. The amount of growth in the tertiary sector is usually measured by the percentage of a country's workforce that it employs.
2. The percentage employed in the different sectors changes as development takes place.

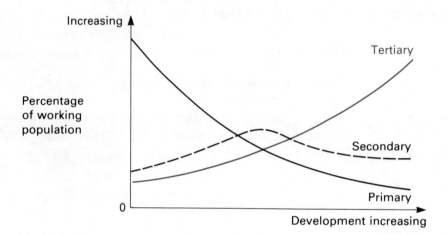

**Figure 13.1** Percentage employed in different sectors of the economy

3. Many developed countries have more than 60% of the working population employed in the tertiary sector while in the least developed countries the figure is often less than 10%.
4. It is sometimes difficult to measure the percentage of tertiary employment in developing countries because many people living in cities have **informal** jobs (e.g. shoe-shines) in the tertiary sector which are not registered but which are estimated to account for 40–60% of a city's workforce.

### (b) Reasons for Growth

1. As the level of development increases the primary and secondary sectors of the economy become more mechanised and create wealth.
2. This causes the growth of the tertiary sector because the increased mechanisation releases people to work in tertiary industry, and the increased wealth creates more demand for services, as people and industry are better able to pay for them.
3. Also as development increases, the amount of time for leisure increases, creating further demand for leisure services.

## 13.3  Location of tertiary industries

### (a) The Location of Tertiary Industry

1. Tertiary industries tend to locate in settlements.
2. The larger the population of the settlement and the richer the area the greater the number, variety and order of tertiary industries.
3. Some of the services within settlements usually have to be visited (e.g. retailing) while others although located in a settlement can be used from a distance (e.g. administration) via the postal, telecommunications and distribution networks.
4. Some tertiary industries are confined mainly to settlements (e.g. retailing) while others serve the whole of a country or region (e.g. postal service).

### (b) Location of Tertiary Industry within Urban Areas

1. The location of tertiary industry within urban areas is not haphazard but forms a pattern.
2. Tertiary industries within urban areas tend to cluster together in the CBD and certain other parts of the urban area (see Section 8.3).

### (c) Reasons for the Location of Tertiary Industry

1. Most tertiary industries are said to be market orientated because their most important locational factor is accessibility to their market, the companies and individual people who want and need to use them.
2. As most of these people and companies are located in major centres of population so are most of the tertiary industries.
3. Large urban areas are most accessible because their transport links, postal and telecommunications services are most efficient. So services that need to be visited and services that are used from a distance can be reached easily.
4. Location in accessible urban areas also allows the large labour force of the tertiary industry to live nearby and have good access to their workplace.
5. Many tertiary industries benefit from agglomeration as they use each other's services and together they form a greater attraction to potential users.

## 13.4  The tourist industry

### (a) The Growth of the Tourist Industry

1. The tourist industry forms the part of the leisure industry concerned with people who are spending one or more nights away from their home for leisure purposes.
2. The tourist industry has grown because the number of people wishing to take holidays has increased as a result of population growth and increased access to holidays.

**Table 13.2** Causes of increased access to holidays

| | |
|---|---|
| Time available | The number of weeks of paid holiday and the percentage of the population who have retired have increased and the average number of hours worked per person has decreased creating a greater demand for tourism. |
| Money available | Average annual wages have increased. |
| Increased car ownership | The percentage of households that have access to a car has increased. This creates flexibility as to where and when people travel making it easier for people to take holidays. |
| Transport developments | The increased efficiency of transport networks has reduced journey times and new links and routes have increased the number of destinations that are available. Transport developments such as charter flights and wide-bodied jets have reduced the relative cost of transport. |

3. The companies that have been created to cater for this demand have encouraged the growth of the industry through advertising and the development of a wide range of alternative holidays to attract as many different sections of the population as possible.
4. Governments have promoted the tourist industry, especially in some developing countries, because the gains that the industry brings to a country can be greater than the losses.

**Table 13.3** The gains and losses of the tourist industry for a country

| Gains | Losses |
|---|---|
| 1. The tourists bring foreign currency into the country. | 1. Money needs to be borrowed abroad; this loan needs to be repaid along with any interest payments if the government is to develop the industry itself*. |
| 2. The tourists buy goods and services from the local people increasing their incomes. | |
| 3. The industry creates jobs. | 2. If a foreign company is used to develop the industry it will take most of the profits out of the country and use some non-local workers*. |
| 4. The government can get more money for development from the increased tax revenue and from the tourists. | 3. Goods may need to be imported to give the tourists the things that they want*. |
| | 4. The environment of the country may be spoiled. |
| | 5. Conflicts may arise between people who want to use a tourist area for industry and the tourists. |
| | 6. Agricultural production may go down as more and more people move to the tourist developments*. |
| | 7. The traditional culture of the area may disappear*. |

*Shows the gains and losses that usually cause concern to only developing countries

192

5. In developed countries many of the costs do not usually apply because the development of the industry is by home-based companies, but the industry still provides foreign currency and creates jobs.

### (b) The Development of Resources for Tourism

1. Resources for tourism can be divided into natural resources and human resources.

**Table 13.4** Some resources for tourism

| Natural resources | Human resources |
|---|---|
| Beaches | Different cultures |
| Warm sea/lakes | Museums |
| Long sunshine hours | Theatres |
| Absence of rain | |
| Beautiful scenery | |
| Different landscapes | |
| Wild animals | |
| Snow-covered slopes | |

2. The tourist industry can be said to be resource orientated as only places that have a suitable resource will be visited.
3. However, while these resources are found in many locations, only those that can be reached will be developed.
4. Development usually involves the creation of places for tourists to stay and the construction of other amenities to increase the appeal of the resource.
5. Where the resource is threatened by tourist developments conservation measures may be taken to ensure that it remains as a resource (e.g. the creation of national parks) reducing some of the losses shown in Table 13.3.
6. Many tourist developments are used only on a seasonal basis.

### (c) The Origin and Destination of Tourists

1. Most tourists originate in the developed countries.
2. Their destination is mainly to tourist locations in the developed countries.
3. An increasing number are travelling from developed countries to developing countries.

## 13.5 Tertiary industry and the environment

See Table 6.3.

## 13.6 Tertiary industry examples

**Table 13.5** Tertiary industry examples

| Named examples of | Factual information needed | Your named example |
| --- | --- | --- |
| 1. A developing country | Name and location, percentage employed in different sectors of the economy and details of the growth of the tertiary sector. | 1. |
| 2. A developed country | Name and location, percentage employed in different sectors of the economy and details of the growth of the tertiary sector. | 2. |
| 3. Tertiary industries (commercial, distribution, public service, personal, public administration) | Name and location. Advantages of location. Details of goods distributed, method of distribution and the customers. | 3.(a)<br>3.(b)<br>3.(c)<br>3.(d)<br>3.(e) |
| 4. Tourist resort in developed country | Name and location. List of developed human and natural resources. Details of the growth in the number of tourists, the origin of tourists and the effects of growth on the area. | 4. |
| 5. Tourist resort in developing country | Name and location. List of developed human and natural resources. Details of the growth in the number of tourists, the origin of the tourists and the effects of growth on the area. | 5. |
| 6. Area of natural beauty used for tourism | Name and location. Detail of the natural resources and their development, the origin and number of visitors and conflicts that exist within the area. | 6. |

# 13.7 Questions and answers

## (a) Structured Questions

### Example 13.1

(a) Look at the figure below:

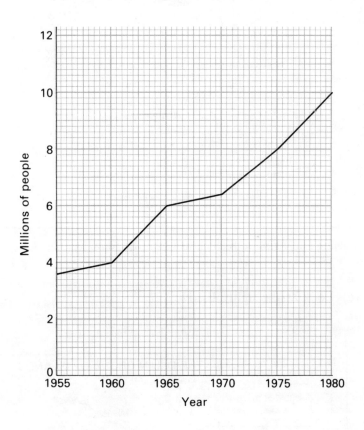

Graph showing the number of UK citizens taking holidays abroad

    (i) Describe the change shown by the graph.
   (ii) Give two reasons to explain this change.

(b) Look at the figure overleaf:

    (i) Choose one economically less developed country which is popular with tourists.
       Mark its position with a cross.
       Write the name of the country.
   (ii) State two reasons why the country you have chosen is popular with tourists.
  (iii) Suggest why country A on the map is not popular with tourists despite being within 6 hours' flying time of much of Europe.
  (iv) How long would it take (approximately) for a tourist to fly from Britain to country B on the map?
   (v) Countries such as India, Bangladesh and Australia are long flight times from Britain but are still visited by many tourists from Britain. Give one reason for this.

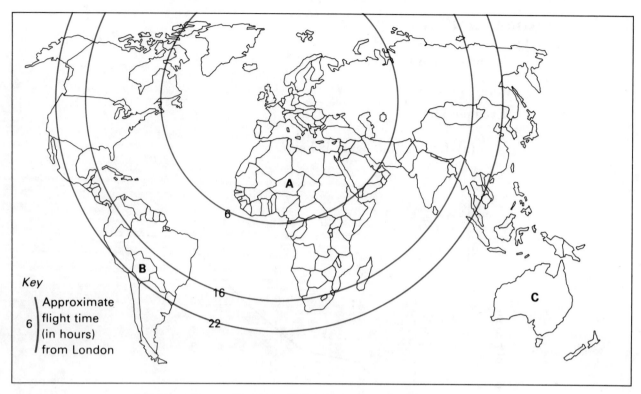

Map showing approximate flight times from London

(c) Look at the figure below:

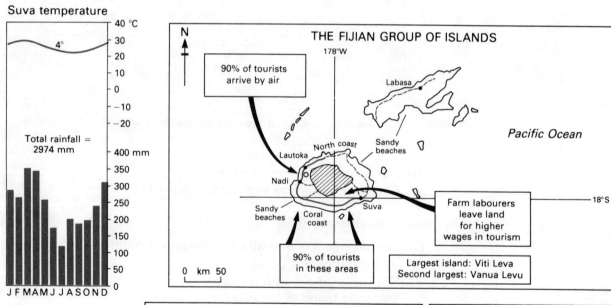

Suva temperature

Total rainfall = 2974 mm

Key
- • Town
- ○ Airport
- —— Tarmac road
- ----- Gravel road
- ▨ Land over 1000 metres

| PURCHASES OF FOOD AND BEVERAGES IN FIJIAN HOTELS | | |
|---|---|---|
| Purchases | Percentage locally produced | Percentage imported |
| Meat/poultry | 41 | 59 |
| Fish/seafood | 46 | 54 |
| Fruit/vegetables | 46 | 54 |
| Bread/dairy products | 86 | 14 |
| Other food | 18 | 82 |
| Beverages | 47 | 63 |
| Cigarettes and tobacco | 88 | 12 |
| Total purchases | 47 | 53 |

| FIJI: SOME EMPLOYMENT STATISTICS | |
|---|---|
| Hotel staff | 3000 people |
| Tourist-related services | 6000 people |
| Construction | 4500 people |

Map and data about the Fijian group of islands

Describe the attractions and/or drawbacks of the Fijian Islands to a tourist from Britain who might be considering spending a holiday there. Use specific information from the figure to support your answer.

(d)    Using the information from the map and the data in the figure:

(i) Describe the likely benefits and problems which the tourist industry has brought to Fiji.
(ii) Imagine you are the Minister for Tourism in Fiji. Describe how you would attempt to overcome the problems outlined in (d) (i).
(NEA syllabus A paper 2 question 3 1988)

**Solution 13.1**

(a)    (i) The number of UK citizens taking holidays abroad has changed, rising from 3.6 million in 1955 to 10 million in 1980.

(ii) **Reason 1**
The cost of holidays abroad has become cheaper when compared with the rise in average earnings, so more people can afford to holiday abroad.
**Reason 2**
The average number of weeks of paid holiday per person has increased, so people have more time to go on holiday.

(b)    (i) See the figure below:

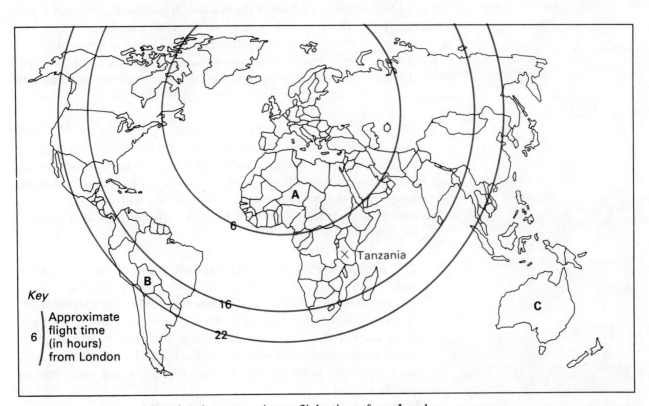

Map showing approximate flight times from London

(ii) **Reason 1**

Tanzania has a different range of tourist facilities (e.g. game reserves).

**Reason 2**

In the summer months when most people take their holiday Tanzania has a low rainfall and high temperatures.

(iii) Country A may not be popular with tourists because it has very few facilities for tourists.

(iv) It would take between 16 and 20 hours to fly to country B.

(v) Many people living in Britain have relatives in these countries whom they want to visit.

(c) **The possible drawbacks**

The journey to the islands will be long and expensive, since they lie 178° west and 18° south. The temperature is constantly between 26 and 30 degrees centigrade which a tourist may find too hot. There is no dry season: the lowest monthly rainfall in July is approximately 129 mm; in the wettest month of February this rises to 350 mm and the yearly total is 2974 mm. This may hinder the leisure activities of the tourists. The road network, on even the main island, consists partly of a gravel road which means that some parts will be inaccessible. In the area which caters for 90% of the tourists there is only one area of sandy beaches, so they may become crowded.

**The possible attractions**

The presence of an airport allows tourists to reach the island quickly. The hot temperatures will allow the tourists to sunbathe, when it is not raining, on the sandy beaches, and to explore the coral coast. The islands offer a variety of environments ranging from the low-lying coast to areas over 1000 m and a chance to explore isolated areas on the north coast of Vitu Levu and the adjoining islands. The tourists will be able to sample a culture and environment different to their own.

(d) (i) The benefits of the tourist industry include the creation of 13 500 jobs directly related to the industry. Also the industry may have created increased demand and employment in agriculture, fishing and the cigarette industry as the products of these industries are bought by the tourist hotels. The tourists will also benefit the islands as they are a source of foreign currency with which to pay for imports.

The problems that the tourist industry brings are that some farm labourers leave the land so agricultural production drops and more food may need to be imported. Also the special needs of the tourists mean 53% of food and beverage purchases have to be imported using valuable foreign currency which could be spent on development projects. The natural environment may have been damaged by the creation of hotels and other tourist facilities.

(ii) I would try to preserve the environment by imposing a limit on the number of tourist developments and any new developments would have to conform to strict planning regulations and be open to comment from the people of the islands.

I would look carefully at the imports used by the tourists and try to begin to produce them in the islands.

Provided that the young farm labourers who are leaving the land are fully employed, I would try to raise the level of agricultural production by introducing appropriate technology.

**Example 13.2**

(a) Study the figure below:

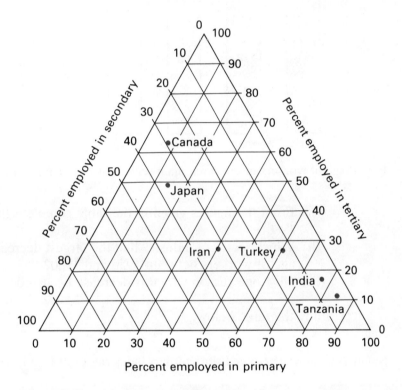

Percentage of workers in each of the three main sectors of industry in selected countries

      (i) What percentage of workers in Canada are employed in secondary industry?
    (ii) Name one country shown on the graph which may be called a 'developing' country.
   (iii) Give one fact shown on the graph to support your choice of that country.

(b) Study the figure below:

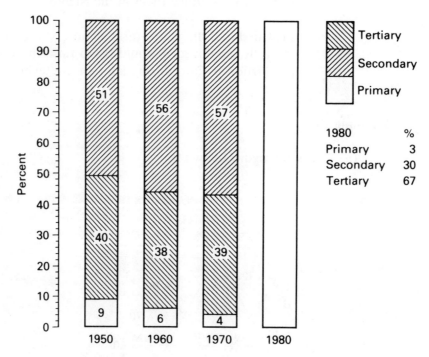

Percentage of workers in the three main sectors of industry in Britain

(i) From the figures given in the table complete the divided bar for 1980.
(ii) Which sector of industry had the largest decrease in the percentage of workers between 1950 and 1980?
(iii) Give one reason why this decrease occurred.

(c) Study the table below:

Numbers employed in some British tertiary industries in 1960 and 1981

| Tertiary industries | Total employed in thousands in 1960 | Rank order | Total employed in thousands in 1981 | Rank order |
|---|---|---|---|---|
| Transport and communications | 1667 | 3 | 1440 | 3 |
| Finance, business and professional | 2575 | | 4928 | |
| Distributive trades | 2870 | | 2635 | |
| Catering and hotels | 592 | | 871 | |

(i) Complete the rank orders on the table above for 1960 and 1981, giving rank 1 to the largest in each year.
(ii) Suggest one reason why the numbers employed in catering and hotels rose between 1960 and 1981.

(**LEAG** syllabus B paper 1 question 3 1988)

**Solution 13.2**

(a)   (i) 30%.
(ii) Tanzania.
(iii) 85% of the workers in Tanzania are employed in the primary sector.

(b)   (i) See the figure below:

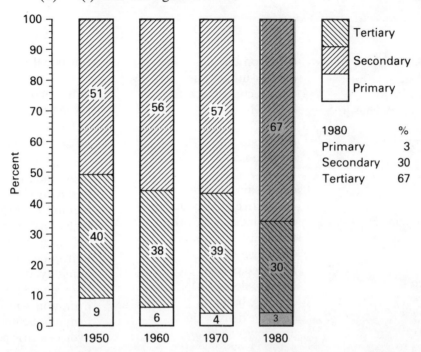

Percentage of workers in the three main sectors of industry in Britain

(ii) The secondary sector.
(iii) The increased use of labour-saving machinery reduced the number of workers that needed to be employed.

(c)   (i) See the table below:

Numbers employed in some British tertiary industries in 1960 and 1981

| Tertiary industries | Total employed in thousands in 1960 | Rank order | Total employed in thousands in 1981 | Rank order |
|---|---|---|---|---|
| Transport and communications | 1667 | 3 | 1440 | 3 |
| Finance, business and professional | 2575 | 2 | 4928 | 1 |
| Distributive trades | 2870 | 1 | 2635 | 2 |
| Catering and hotels | 592 | 4 | 871 | 4 |

(ii) The increase in leisure time between 1960 and 1981 is one reason for the increased demand for catering services and hotels. To meet this increased demand more people have become employed in this type of tertiary industry.

# Index

life expectancy 90
link 139
load 50

magma 15
Malthus 88
mantle *13*
mass movement 46
meander *54*
Mercalli Scale 19
metamorphic rock 14
migration 89
mode 142
multi-lateral aid 124
multi-national company 124, 175
multiplier effect 127

natural gas *75*
natural increase 88
natural resources 74
neocolonialism 124
node 139
non-renewable resources 74
nucleated pattern *103*

occluded front *31*
ocean currents 33
ocean ridge *16, 26*
ocean trench *26*
oil *75*
omnivore 35
optimum conditions 160
origin *19*
out-migration 89
outer core *13*
overland flow *48, 49*
overpopulation 88
oxidation *46*

pastoral farming 158
percolation *48, 49*
pollution 77
population cycle *89*
population density 87

population distribution 87
population pyramid 91, *93*, *95*
population structure 91
precipitation 30
pressure gradient 30
primary industry 157
primary producer 35
pull factor 91
push factor 91

quartenary industry 189

rain gauge *29*
range *103*
redevelopment 108
refurbishment 108
regime *53*
renewable resources 74
Richter Scale 19
rift valley *16*
rock fall 47
Rostow 125

saltation *50*
sectors of the economy *190*
sedimentary rock 14
seismic focus *19*
seismometer 19
service industry 189
settlement form 102
settlement function 102
settlement hierarchy *103*, 103
settlement site 102
settlement situation 102
shanty town *107*
sial *14*
sill *22, 23*
sima *14*
site and services scheme *107*
soil creep 47
soil erosion 55
solifluction 47
solution *50*
sphere of influence *103*

stem flow *48, 49*
storm surge 35
stream order *49*
subduction zone 15
subsistence farming 158
sunshine recorder *29*
suspension *50*

terrace *54*
tertiary industry 189
thermometer *29*
threshold population *103*
throughflow *48, 49*
topological map 139
tornado 35
traction *50*
transition zone *105*
transpiration *48*
tributary *49*
tropical cyclone 35
tsunamis 20
twilight zone *105*
typhoon 35

underpopulation 88
uranium *75*
urban field *103*
urban sprawl 108
urbanisation 102

vertical-integration 175
volcanic features 18
volcano 18
voluntary aid 124
voluntary migrant 91

warm front *31*
warm sector *31*
waterfall *54*
watershed 48, *49*
weathering 46
wetted perimeter *51*
wine vane *29*

yield 160

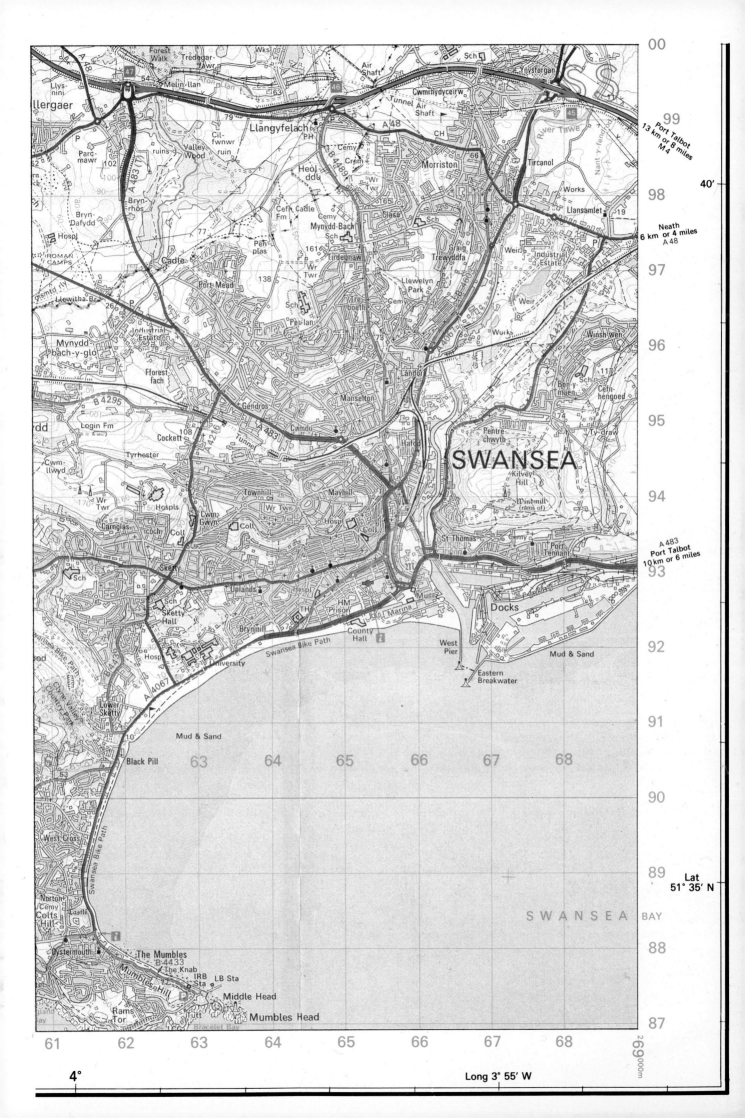